AWARD WINNING ARCHITECTURE
INTERNATIONAL YEARBOOK 1998/99

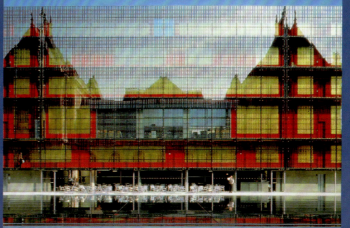

International Yearbook

Award Winning Architecture

1998/99

Edited by
Frantisek D. Sedlacek

in cooperation with
Christine Waiblinger-Jens

Prestel Munich · London · New York

COMPREHENSIVE LISTING

INDEXES

Hic Rhodus, Hic Salta

To Lucie, Jana, Martin

In the beginning was the word—not only in the Bible, but probably at the beginning of all activities, and especially all intellectual movements and trends.

Today, the magical word at the beginning of everything is "globalization", although it is not entirely new nor is it unknown. In the past, one spoke of "internationalism" instead of "globalization".

For the normal person in normal life, this phenomenon began much earlier; and it began gradually and unnoticed. It all started with food, it would seem, though not with the fast food, soft drinks, candy bars, chewing gum, cigarettes and pizzas of our own generation. The refined form of internationalism of our grandparents' age manifested itself through things like whisky, champagne, caviar and cigars and knew no geographical boundaries. Luxury is and always will be international. For that reason, it is of little relevance in this context. What is important in making any judgement is the opinion of the masses, and not of a thin social stratum. Just as the evening dress and the obligatory white tie and tails came to represent a standard throughout the world, so today true internationalization has been accomplished in the form of jeans. In my generation, internationalization was closely—and probably quite accurately—identified with Americanization; but there was never any danger of monotonous uniformity.

The adepts of internationalism were a progressive minority of individualists who willingly allowed the regionally oriented majority latitude for local development. Globalization, however, has a quite different focus. It wants everything; it wants to dominate us, with no exceptions, no international pluralism, no regionalism. Otherwise we shall not be able to survive. The world is indeed developing in a direction in which national boundaries are disappearing. But do we really want a world in which there are no barriers, no cultural boundaries?

The current political, economic and administrative union that is taking place in my home—Europe—has certainly increased the feeling for cultural differences. The nations of Europe are all clearly differentiated from each other and form distinct entities with their own histories, mentalities and characters. It is an exciting adventure to get to know and to understand the different experiences that underlie different cultures—all the more so, since the individual nations are further subdivided into regions, all of which function as independent cultural microcosms. I hope—indeed, I am sure—that the same applies to other continents. It should also apply to architecture, which should continue to grow from local structures and resist global conformity and regimentation. Under no circumstances may it end in provinciality, though. It is important to be acquainted with international culture and to translate it into regional facts in such a way that it may continue to develop in its own way, and be refined—not just conform.

That confronts us with the first problem. What is a region today? Southern England and northern England, or England as a whole?

Smaller, larger or even greater geographical entities, such as continents; or just east, west, north and south? A further problem lies in determining where positive internationalization ends and the negative globalization of architecture begins.

The Bauhaus was certainly international—and good. A Swedish furniture concern is attempting to globalize interior design in the home, and the effect cannot automatically be condemned as bad. What is involved here is culture, architecture as art, and what happens when these elements are globalized. Some of the symptoms are truly disturbing. Architectural space is being transformed into a leisure landscape for the consumer society. The arts, including architecture, globally forgo a possible further dimension in order to remain globally attractive. The intelligent buildings of globalized architecture present themselves as "action architecture", as "events architecture" that has a broad appeal and provides a wide range of experiences. Architecture of this kind is entertaining, easily digestible, and has a profile geared to market requirements, as if it had been designed by the advertising strategists at company headquarters rather than by architects. Globalized architecture is, therefore, expected to be globally applicable.

The concept of seeking a relation to the locality is out of date. The topos —the thematic dialogue between architecture and its location, which in the past was a guarantee of uniqueness—is no longer a criterion. This is understandable in an age in which architecture is finally losing its ability to reflect social conditions. It is understandable in an age in which a concrete, built location in a local world is frequented, sought out and loved largely by children, the underprivileged or the socially weak. It is understandable in an age in which the cultivated modern human being—despite all protests to the contrary—is really turning away from nature and leading a life that is more and more abstract, less and less related to a specific place.

To experience a bank building in Istanbul as different from one in Tokyo or New York is probably really anachronistic, although it might just be regarded as acceptable. What is frightening, however, is when the same criteria are meant to apply to housing developments around the world. What do I wish to achieve? What do I expect? What am I advocating? That can be stated and defined quite simply.

The days increase in intensity, with documents pouring in from all over the world, containing descriptions of outstanding, prizewinning objects for this book. One opens the envelopes with great joy, with enormous expectations and a certain proud ceremony. What awaits us? With great relief, one can say they are, on the whole, good; some are better than others; and there are even some very good works of architecture among them. At the same time, one notes with interest that corrugated sheet metal façades, for example, are suddenly "out" worldwide and wood is "in". Unfortunately, after a while—or after a certain quantity—it is difficult to distinguish from which country or continent the various objects come,

to which culture they belong. They are all good; they are all similar; indeed, they are all of the same kind.

Architecture is becoming globalized.

For me, that is a sign that the globalized globe really is round. Later, one investigates the envelopes to find out where the various projects come from. But note: it is not the senders' addresses that are interesting; it is the stamps I look at. They have not been globalized yet. Not only is the name of each country printed on them unmistakably in words. It is also clearly identifiable and decipherable from the graphics. This is probably because the stamps are a cultural asset used by all strata of society in the country in question—everyone, not just a select few who find them beautiful. Last, but not least, for the rest of the world the stamps represent a specific country and the political, economic and cultural conditions prevailing in its society.

It would be desirable if architecture, too, were to retain its own unmistakable qualities. Despite internationalization, globalization and most probably universalization in the future, it would be better if the architectural globe were not quite so round, but had more local corners and contours.

Frantisek D. Sedlacek
Editor

Notes on the Third Volume of this Yearbook

AWA Award Winning Architecture—International Yearbook 1998/99 is the third annual review to be published in this series.

In this new volume, we again present buildings from throughout the world which have been awarded official prizes by the various national architects' organizations as the best schemes of the year. Prizes of this kind, awarded by architects to architects, are the most important national distinctions of all, since they are based on objective expert opinions and not on commercial considerations.

AWA 1998/99, therefore, presents a complete review of the most interesting and exciting—in other words, the best—new buildings in the world today.

For anyone who chooses to divide the current of time into such tiny units as a year, it is impossible to sit back and contemplate the success of the previous year's volume—which has just appeared—with a sense of smug satisfaction. The success of the first two yearbooks has encouraged us to present an even greater number of prizewinning schemes. A closer collaboration with the architects themselves and with the relevant professional bodies has enabled us to compile a comprehensive review of international prizewinning architecture. This year, in addition to the schemes that have been honoured by the national organizations, we are presenting the winners of other awards such as prizes from regional bodies. We have used the year, therefore, to take account of this new situation, and we have developed and modified our concept in order to present more information in this third yearbook and to do so in a more memorable form.

The review contains an even greater number of buildings in the coloured project section than in previous years. At the same time, we are omitting the illustrations in the so-called listings section. The aim of presenting as broad a spectrum as possible can be achieved only by applying strict selection criteria. Despite a great interest in form, we did not set a purely aesthetic standard. The terms of reference are far wider and include internationality, variety and above all the spirit of innovation.

This edition of the Award Winning Architecture yearbook is devoted almost exclusively to recently completed buildings that are also fine examples of modern architecture and that therefore—in addition to their publication in the specialist press—deserve wider recognition through a work of this kind.

In our opinion, the architectural projects published in AWA 1998/99 radiate an optimistic vigour, despite the problems that exist in the present difficult economic situation.

We should like to extend our thanks to the various professional organizations that have again worked in close collaboration with us to enable their award-winning schemes to appear in this unique international context. In many cases, these bodies informed us immediately after the prize-giving ceremonies of the projects their juries had selected, thus allowing the work to be presented in a comprehensive form and to its best advantage.

The somewhat modified layout, which is now divided up under various "headings"; the more elaborate design with a hard cover and dust jacket; and the clearer presentation of the projects—each with a two-page spread—are in keeping with the quantity and quality of the schemes presented.

To make this volume easier to use, the prizewinners are not grouped according to their countries of origin or the places where they work, but according to the countries that awarded the prizes.

Finally, we should like to thank all the architects who made this publication possible by sending us their work, includng those prizewinners whose schemes could unfortunately be mentioned only in the listings section for the reasons given above.

We hope we may continue to count on the vital support of all participants in the future, for only with their help is it possible to produce a yearbook as comprehensive as AWA 1998/99, with the present range of contents and production quality.

Christine Waiblinger-Jens

Foreword

Around the world, architecture is becoming more adventurous and innovative. In three dimensions and on a colossal scale, architects are achieving what painters and sculptors set out to do in the early decades of this century—to play with abstract forms and shapes and blocks of colour, and to experiment with expressive, curvaceous, sculptural form. Russian Constructivism is being followed by modern Deconstruction. The essence of innovation is freedom and an openness of mind. This means not only the often repeated freedom of the artist or designer, but freedom for the client as well. For the client, freedom means choice—freely choosing the architect whose work he or she likes, and, no less important, the architect with whom he or she feels a rapport. It also means freedom to choose, or evolve, the type or form of building he or she wants, without the pre-constraints of prevailing tastes or philosophies.

There signs that, with globalisation, a new orthodoxy is on the rise. Post-Modernism, though it produced a great many buildings that were unattractive, had a liberating effect, encouraging architects to look back, forward and sideways, to play with volumes, to delight in mass and colour, and use decoration in novel ways.

Orthodoxy comes in many forms. First, it most obviously comes in the tyranny of fashion, to which architecture, and architects, are disturbingly prone. The 1996 Venice Biennale showed this only too clearly with one national pavilion after another exhibiting fashionable Deconstruction. The tyranny of fashion is quite simply the dominance of a particular look. More insidious, and no less frequent in the history of architecture over the last five hundred years, is the tyranny of doctrine. I often wonder what the virtuoso Gothic masons and carvers who produced the explosion of creativity we call Perpendicular or Flamboyant at the end of the Middle Ages thought about the sudden imposition of a rigid new classical vocabulary and grammar.

When the architect-earl Lord Burlington established the Palladian ascendancy in England early in the 18th century, the poet Alexander Pope retorted, "My Lord, your just and noble rules, will fill the land with imitating fools". Today we have manufactured a new set of labels of derision and hate. Prime among them are Disney and "Disneyfying"— forgetting that the Disney Corporation is a major patron of adventurous new architecture (Isozaki, Gehry et al.).

The Disney label is applied to anything that it seen as *ersatz* or fake rather than "pure" and "honest". This ignores the fact that much fine architecture through the ages has been theatrical in nature, whether presenting a single show front to the world or indulging in deliberate visual trickery or *trompe l'oeil*.

The battle cry for the creation of an "architecture of our time" rings around the world. No less important is an architecture with a sense of place. This does not mean slavish adherence to traditional forms, materials and techniques but an understanding of volume, both internal and external, of the relation of window to wall, of roof pitches, of features such as balconies and courtyards, of the play of light and shade not only on facades but within buildings—the whole indoor-outdoor relationship which is crucial to all architecture.

We talk of beauty in architecture as an ideal, forgetting sometimes that fine, or striking, looks in buildings, as well people (or animals), can come in forms quite different from the conventionally handsome or pretty. To Beauty, I would add first of all the Sublime, the Magical and the Grotesque. The Escorial, Philip II's great palace monastery, is not beautiful; rather it is austere to the extreme, but also awesome, august and infinitely imposing. The philosopher Edmund Burke listed the qualities of the Sublime as Obscurity, Power, Privations, Vastness, Infinity, Succession and Uniformity. These are the qualities of much industrial architecture from the warehouses of maritime cities to the blast furnaces of the Ruhr. Mass and volume are qualities in architecture as enduring as lightness and transparency. As the great master of English baroque, Sir John Vanbrugh, stated wittily: "Lie lightly on him earth, tho' he laid many a load on thee".

The Magical in architecture is expressed through silhouettes and through festive qualities, particularly at night. The early skyscrapers in Manhattan or Chicago are obvious 20th-century examples, as are many cinemas and theatres. The new transparency in architecture, where walls of glass light lofty internal spaces, allows buildings to glow from within, without the need for conventional floodlighting. The Grotesque brings elements of the bizarre and the exotic, and above all surprise, into architecture.

Nor in this age of Minimalism should splendor, one of the oldest attributes of architecture, be forgotten. An old socialist hymn puts it well: "They shall be simple in their lives/But splendid in their public ways". International Modernism changed the relation between architecture and the other arts, particularly the decorative arts and crafts. With the call of 1% for art, the emphasis has been initially on freestanding sculptures and paintings. Now there is a welcome trend to integrate art into building and to broaden the definition of art to include elements such as stained glass, furniture and fittings and stone carving. Now its the time for architects to once again look at decorative painting and stucco.

The task of a book such as this, from one year to the next, is to show whether world architecture is treading a wide and varied path full of surprises or whether a new uniformity is once again on the rise. The virtue of including prize winning designs from all over the world is that there is something unexpected for everyone.

Marcus Binney

**DETAILED DESCRIPTIONS
OF SELECTED PROJECTS:
A REPRESENTATIVE CROSS-SECTION**

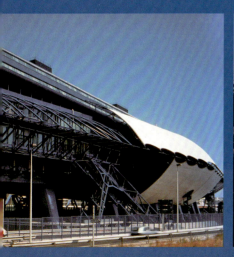

**Lawrence Nield and Partners Australia
in Association with John Mainwaring
& Associates Pty. Ltd., Noosa Heads
Sunshine Coast University College Library**

Sippy Downs, Sunshine Coast, Queensland, Australia
August 1995–January 1997

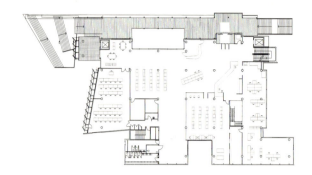

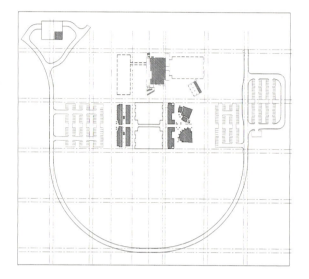

Award   Sir Zelman Cowen Award for Public Buildings
Given by   RAIA The Royal Australian Institute of Architects
Prize Presentation   November/14/1997
Members of the Jury   John Castles, Ed Haysom, Virginia Kerridge,
   Peter Parkinson, Betty Churcher
Design Team   Lawrence Nield, Neil Hanson, Annabel Lahz,
   John Mainwaring, Joanne Case
Structural Engineering   Taylor Thomson Whitting,
   Mc Williams Consulting Engineers (Site Supervision)
Mechanical Engineering   Lincolne Scott Australia Pty. Ltd.
Electrical Engineering   Lincolne Scott Australia Pty. Ltd.
Air Conditioning Consultant   Lincolne Scott Australia Pty. Ltd.
Lighting Consultant   Lincolne Scott Australia Pty. Ltd.
Interior Design   John Mainwaring & Associates Pty. Ltd. – AHA Design
Landscape Architecture   John Mongard
Quantity Surveying   Graham Lukins & Partners
Approximate Cost   A$ 5,200,000
Site Area   4,000 m²
Building Area   3,500 m²
Total Floor Area   3,000 m²
Photographer   John Gollings, Jon Linkins
Further Reading   Australian Architect, May/June 1997
   and November/December 1997

Elena Neururer-Theodorou, Alois Neururer, Vienna
Hotel Klinglhuber

Krems, Austria
1994–1996

Award   Staatspreis 1996 für Wirtschaftsbauten: Tourismus und Architektur
Given by   Bundesministerium für wirtschaftliche Angelegenheiten
Prize Presentation   October/27/1996
Members of the Jury   Derek Linstrum, Manfred Wehdorn, Jürgen Bauer,
   Rainer Schauer, Erich Musyl, Karl Fiala, Paul Schimka, Christian Knöbl
Design Team   Elena Neururer-Theodorou, Alois Neururer, Stella Kontou,
   Boris Braunschmid
Civil Engineering   Werner Retter, Krems
Lighting Consultant   Jakob Uhl, Vienna
Interior Design   Elena Neururer-Theodorou, Alois Neururer
Quantity Surveying   Alois Neururer
Approximate Cost   ÖS 20,000,000
   (ÖS 25,000,000 Including Furnishing and Payments)
Site Area   990 m²
Building Area   510 m²
Total Floor Area   1,970 m²
Photographer   Margherita Spiluttini, Vienna
Further Reading   Waechter-Böhm, Lisbeth: Neururer & Neururer,
   Schlichtheit währt am längsten, In: Architektur Aktuell 198/1996, pp.74–78

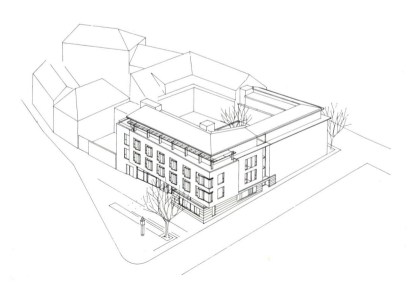

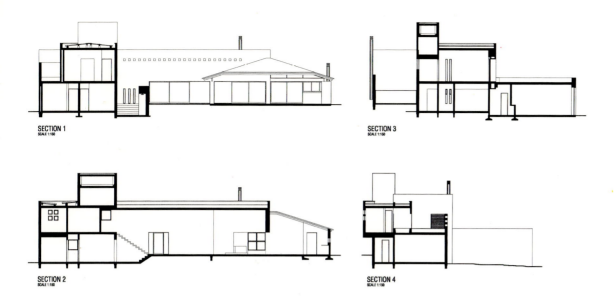

SECTION 1
SCALE 1:150

SECTION 3
SCALE 1:150

SECTION 2
SCALE 1:150

SECTION 4
SCALE 1:150

Henrique de Castro Reinach, Maurício Menezes Mendonça
Sacha's House

Piracaia, São Paulo, Brazil
1995–1997

Award   Prêmio IAB/SP 1996
Given by   IAB Instituto de Arquitetos do Brasil, Departamento São Paulo
Prize Presentation   June/17/1997
Members of the Jury   Abrahão Sanovicz, José Maggalhaes Junior,
   Sylvio Barros Sawaya
Design Team   Alexandre Effori de Mello, Cristina Boggi, Felipe Rodrigues de
   Almeida, Flavia Cancian, Gustavo Viana, Lemy Tanabe, Mirelle Alves da Silva,
   Patricia de Castro Cardoso, Ricardo Bellio
Structural Engineering   Heloisa Martins Maringoni
Lighting Consultant   Stiller, Franco & Fortes Consultores S/C Ltda.
   Lighting Design/Arquitetura
Interior Design   Reinach Mendonça Arquitetos Associados S/C Ltda.
Approximate Cost   US$ 200,000
Site Area   10,000 m²
Building Area   310 m²
Total Floor Area   350 m²
Photographer   Henrique de Castro Reinach
Further Reading   Projeto/Design, August 1997, Revista de Arquitetura,
   Interiores e Design, Arco Editorial São Paulo

Paulo Henrique Paranhos
Espaço Cultural de Palmas

Palmas, Brazil
April 1994–November 1996

Award   Prêmio III. Jovens de Arquitetura 1997
Given by   IAB Instituto de Arquitetos do Brasil
Prize Presentation   July/14/1997
Members of the Jury   André Vainer, Antônio Carlos Sant'Anna,
    Décio Tozzi, João Walter Toscano, José Carlos Ribeiro de Almeida
Design Team   Tao Arquitetura
Structural Engineering   Alex Fernandes
Civil Engineering   Alex Fernandes
Electrical Engineering   J. Maciel
Acoustic Engineering   Roberto Thompson Motta
Air Conditioning Consultant   Projetherm Engenharia
Lighting Consultant   Roberto Thompsom Motta
Interior Design   Paulo Henrique Paranhos
Landscape Architecture   Prefeitura Municipal de Palmas
Quantity Surveying   Prefeitrua Municipal de Palmas
Approximate Cost   US$ 3,000,000
Site Area   30,000 m²
Building Area   9,440 m²
Photographer   Paulo Henrique Paranhos, F. Mitt, Edson Lopes
Further Reading   Revista a+u, no. 76, Brazil

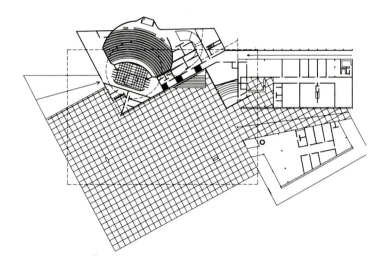

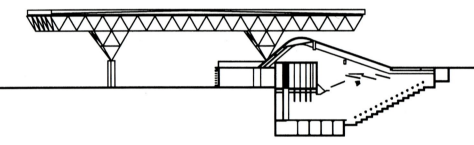

Schmidt, Hammer & Lassen A/S, Århus
Katuaq Cultural Center Greenland

Nuuk, Greenland
1994–1997

Award Aereskalejdoskop 1996
Given by DAL Danske Arkitekters Landsforbund,
  Akademisk Arkitektforening
Prize Presentation September 1996
Design Team Schmidt, Hammer & Lassen
Structural Engineering Abrahamsen & Nielsen
Civil Engineering Rambøll (Site Manager), Nuuk, Greenland
Electrical Engineering Rambøll, Århus
Acoustic Engineering Jorgen Heiden – Rambøll, Århus
Air Conditioning Consultant Rambøll – Tnerkild Petersen, Århus
Lighting Consultant Gobo Lighting/Andersen & Co., Århus
Interior Design Schmidt, Hammer & Lassen
Supervision Architectural Works Tegnestuen Nuuk A/S,
  Nuuk, Greenland
Approximate Cost DKR 91,000,000
Total Floor Area 3,900 m²
Photographer Peter Barfoed

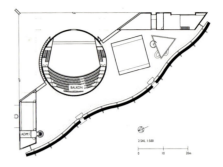

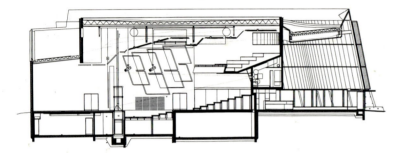

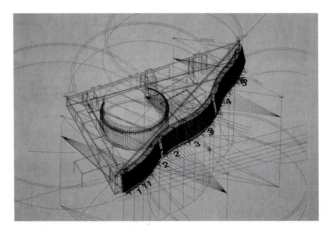

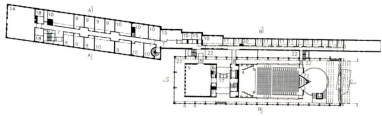

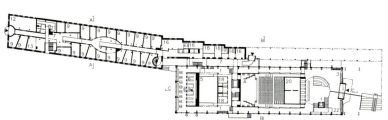

Ola Laiho, Mikko Pulkkinen, Ilpo Raunio, Turku
Turku Music Conservatory

Turku, Finland
1992–1994

Award   Suomi Palkinto
Given by   Valtion Rakennustaidetoimikunta
Prize Presentation   December/12/1996
Members of the Jury   Tore Tallqvist, Maija Kairamo, Pekka Laatio,
  Marja-Riitta Norri, Jorma Panu, Marita Suikki, Kai Wartiainen
Structural Engineering   Turun Juva Oy
Civil Engineering   Turun Juva Oy
Mechanical Engineering   Insinööritoimisto Juhani Lehtonen Oy
Electrical Engineering   Insinööritoimisto Juhani Lehtonen Oy
Acoustic Engineering   Suomen Akustiikkakeskus Oy
Approximate Cost   FIM 60,000,000
Site Area   4,815 m²
Building Area   3,363 m²
Total Floor Area   7,998 m²
Photographer   Ola Laiho
Further Reading   Glasforum 6/1995; Arkkitehti 5–6/1995

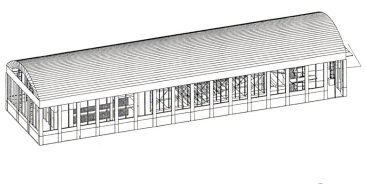

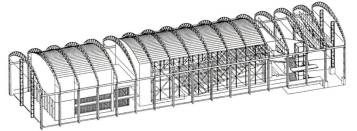

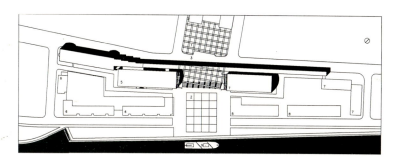

Joseph Almudever et Christian Lefebvre, Toulouse
Centre Regional de la Propriété Forestière Auzeville

Auzeville-Tolosane, France

Award   Prix AMO 1996
Given by   AMO Architecture et Maîtres d'Ouvrage
Prize Presentation   March/26/1997
Members of the Jury   Jacques Rigaud, Claude Cagol, Paul Chemetov,
   Pierre Ecoiffier, Jean-Marie Esnault, Thérèse Evette, Serge Grzybowski,
   Francois Guy, Alain Jacob de Cordemoy, Bertrand Lemoine, Michel Macary,
   Wladimir Mitrofanoff, Philippe Motte, Jean-Philippe Ricard, Henri Rouilleault
Structural Engineering   Bet Deberdt, Foix
Electrical Engineering   Bet Trouvin, Toulouse
Air Conditioning Consultant   Bet Trouvin
Interior Design   Almudever & Lefebvre
Landscape Architecture   Almudever & Lefebvre
Approximate Cost   FF 3,400,0000
Site Area   4,000 m²
Building Area   600 m²
Total Floor Area   600 m²
Photographer   Studio Ze, Toulouse
Further Reading   Arca International, no. 6, Septembre 1997

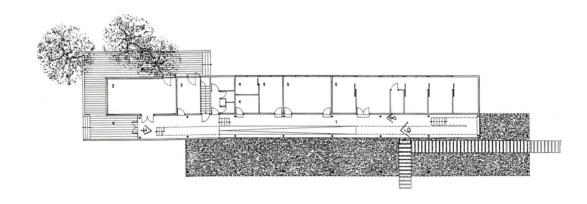

Dominique Coulon, Strasbourg
Collège Pasteur

Strasbourg, France

Design and Construction Period   1995–1996
Award   Prix de la Première Oeuvre
Given by   Le Moniteur
Prize Presentation   January/12/1998
Members of the Jury   Alain Granjean, Pierre-Louis Faloci,
   Aurélio Galfetti, Sébastian Redecke, Jacques Lucan, Dominique Boudet
Design Team   M. Bayer, J. Richter (Assistant Architect)
Structural Engineering   Paul-Henry Huchard TETRA et OTH
Electrical Engineering   OTH
Acoustic Engineering   Bruit Son Musique
Life Safety Consultant   C2BI
Landscape Architecture   Pascale Richter
Quantity Surveying   OTH
Approximate Cost   FF 30,000,000 (Tax not included)
Site Area   10,000 m²
Building Area   5,800 m²
Total Floor Area   2,200 m²
Photographer   Jean Marie Monthiers, Hervé Dabadie, Willaume & Testu

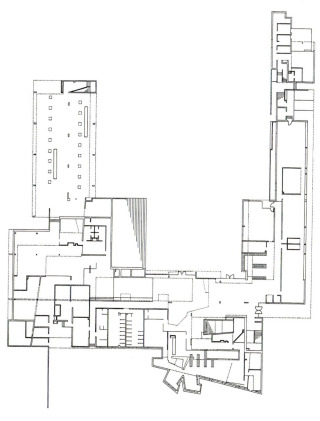

**Agence Franc – Gérard Franc,
Jean-Claude Chauvidon, Paris
Usine Axe**

Saint-Désir-de-Lisieux, France

Design and Construction Period   1992–1995
Award   Prix AMO 1996
Given by   AMO Architecture et Maîtres d'Ouvrage
Prize Presentation   March/26/1997
Members of the Jury   Jacques Rigaud, Claude Cagol, Paul Chemetov,
   Pierre Ecoiffier, Jean-Marie Esnault, Thérèse Evette, Serge Grzybowski,
   François Guy, Alain Jacob de Cordemoy, Bertrand Lemoine, Michel Macary,
   Wladimir Mitrofanoff, Philippe Motte, Jean-Philippe Ricard, Henri Rouilleault
Design Team   Agence Franc
All Engineering   Agence Franc
Interior Design   Agence Franc
Lighting Consultant   Agence Franc
Landscape Architecture   Agence Franc
Quantity Surveying   Agence Franc
Approximate Cost   FF 16,000,000
Site Area   20,000 m²
Building Area   6,300 m²
Total Floor Area   7,300 m²
Photographer   Franck Castel
Further Reading   Le Moniteur, Architecture – AMC, February 1997

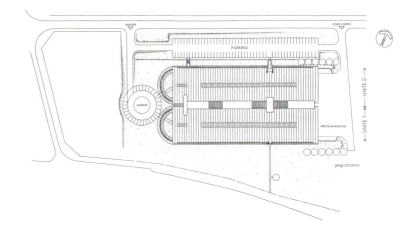

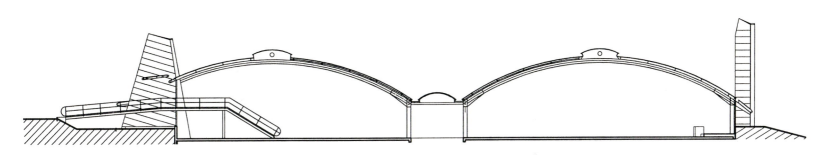

Jean-Marc Ibos and Myrto Vitart, Paris
The Fine Arts Museum of Lille

Lille, France
1990–1997

Award   Prix de l'Equerre d'Argent
Given by   Le Moniteur
Prize Presentation   January/12/1998
Members of the Jury   Alain Granjean, Pierre-Louis Faloci,
   Aurélio Galfetti, Sébastian Redecke, Jacques Lucan, Dominique Boudet
Structural Engineering   Khephren Ingénierie, Y.R.M. Anthony Hunt Associates
   (Façades Consultant)
Civil Engineering   Khephren Ingénierie
Mechanical Engineering   Alto Ingénierie
Electrical Engineering   Alto Ingénierie
Acoustic Engineering   Peutz + Associés
Air Conditioning Consultant   Alto Ingénierie
Lighting Consultant   L'Observatoire 1, Georges Berne
Life Safety Consultant   Cabinet Casso & Cie
Interior Design   Jean-Marc Ibos and Myrto Vitart
Landscape Architecture   Louis Benech
Quantity Surveying   Atec
Approximate Cost   FF 180,000,000
Site Area   13,500 m²
Building Area   8,750 m²
Photographer   Georges Fessy, Paris
Further Reading   Le Moniteur Architecture – A.M.C.,
   September 1997, No 82, pp. 23–35

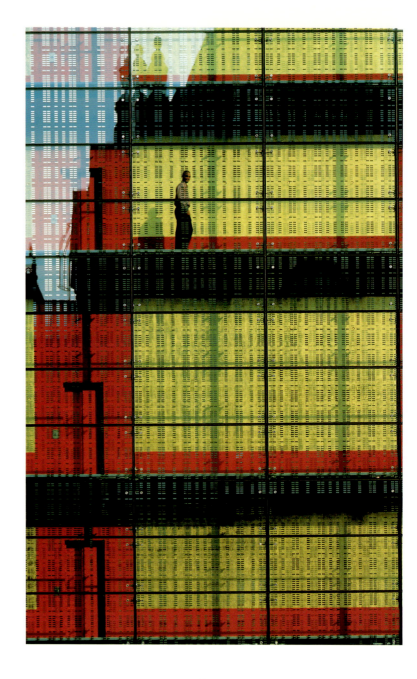

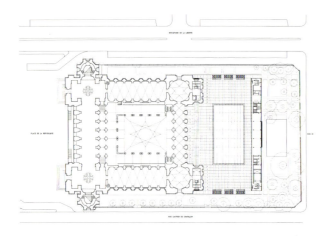

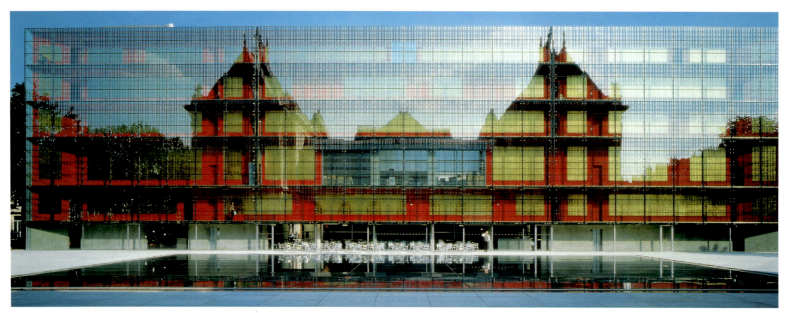

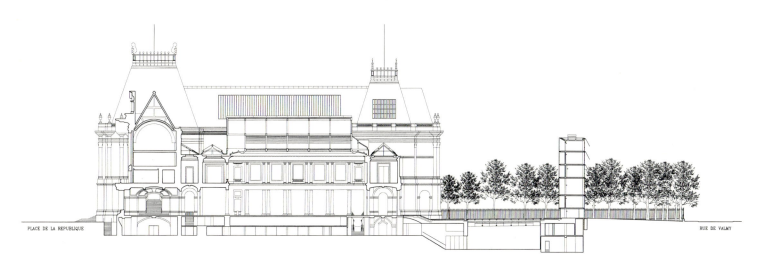

PLACE DE LA REPUBLIQUE   RUE DE VALMY

Tadao Ando, Osaka, Japan, and Günter Pfeifer, Lörrach, Germany
Vitra Conference Pavilion

Weil am Rhein, Germany
1989–1993

Award Hugo-Häring-Preis 1997 des BDA Baden-Württemberg
Given by BDA Bund Deutscher Architekten Baden-Württemberg
Prize Presentation October/14/1997
Members of the Jury Karl Baumschlager, Gerhart Laage, Eberhardt Palmer,
  Matthias Sauerbruch, Michael Schumacher, Rudolf Stegers
Project Architect Hiromitsu Kuwata
Project Management Günter Pfeifer and Roland Mayer – GPF & Assoziierte,
  Lörrach
Project Leader Peter M. Bährle
Photographer vitra.

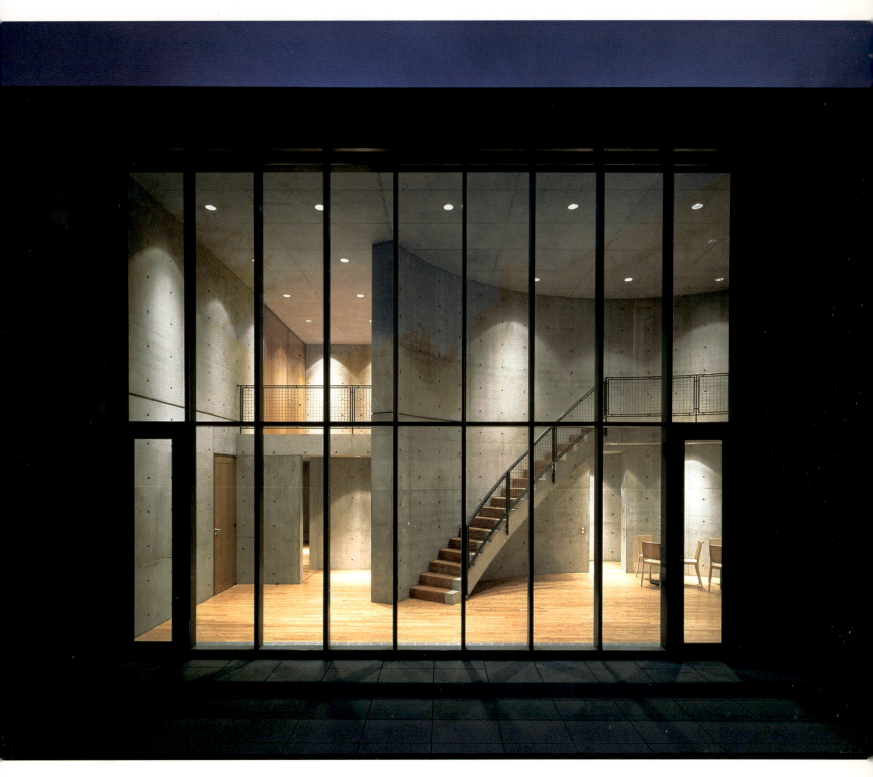

Werner Bäuerle, Konstanz
Duplex Söhnckestrasse, Munich-Solln

Munich, Germany
1996–1997

Award BDA Preis Bayern 1997
Given by BDA Bund Deutscher Architekten Bayern
Prize Presentation February/3/1998
Members of the Jury Eric Adlercreutz, Jan Gezelius, Peter Kulka,
 Gerhard Matzig, Gerhard Spangenberg
Design Team Helmut Fischer, Bad Endorf
Site Area 951 m²
Building Area 354 m²
Total Floor Area 550 m²
Photographer Stefan Müller-Naumann, Munich

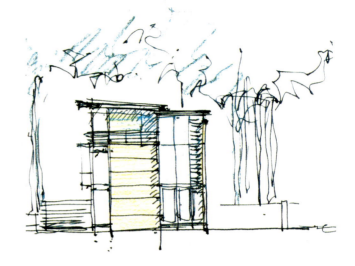

BauCoop Cologne – Wolfgang Felder, Cologne
Industrial Park Nordstern

Gelsenkirchen, Germany
1994–1997

Award   Constructec-Preis 1998 (Special Award)
Given by   Deutsche Messe AG with BDA Bund Deutscher Architekten
Prize Presentation   April/21/1998
Members of the Jury   Françoise Hélène Jourda, Jürgen Bredow,
    Klaus Daniels, Dieter Eberle, Ingeborg Flagge, Nicola Fortmann-Drühe,
    Karl Ganser, Theo Hotz, Helmut C. Schulitz, Werner Schumann
Design Team   BauCoop Cologne – Wolfgang Felder
Structural Engineering   Konstruktionsgruppe für Bauwesen, Cologne
Civil Engineering   Konstruktionsgruppe für Bauwesen, Cologne
Electrical Engineering   Elektro Meißner, Industriemontage GmbH, Odenthal
Environmental Engineering   Büro K.J. Heinrichs, Kerpen
Air Conditioning Consultant   Burkamp + Meißner, Arnsberg
Lighting Consultant   Burkamp + Meißner, Arnsberg
Life Safety Consultant   BauCoop Cologne – Wolfgang Felder
Interior Design   BauCoop Cologne – Wolfgang Felder
Landscape Architecture   Bundesgartenschau Gelsenkirchen
Quantity Surveying   BauCoop Cologne – Wolfgang Felder
Approximate Cost   DM 15,213,450
Site Area   8,700 m²
Building Area   5,120 m²
Total Floor Area   11,720 m²
Photographer   Lukas Roth, Cologne
Further Reading   Centrum, Jahrbuch Architektur und Stadt, 1997–1998

Baumschlager & Eberle, Lochau, Austria
Building for Bearing Technology
Wolfurt, Austria
February 1993–August 1996

Award   Constructec-Preis 1996 (Special award)
Given by   Deutsche Messe AG with BDA Bund Deutscher Architekten
Prize Presentation   June/19 /1996
Members of the Jury   Thomas Herzog, Mels Crouwel,
    Klaus Daniels, Dörte Gatermann, Jesper Gottlieb, Sepp D. Heckmann,
    Andreas Gottlieb Hempel, Bernd Steigerwald, Frank Werner
Design Team   Architekturbüro Baumschlager & Eberle, Lochau, Austria
Structural Engineering   Ernst Mader
Mechanical Engineering   GMI-Ingenieure
Electrical Engineering   Ingenieure Gmeiner
Acoustic Engineering   Zumbach, Switzerland
Interior Design   Baumschlager & Eberle, Lochau, Austria
Landscape Architecture   Baumschlager & Eberle, Lochau, Austria
Quantity Surveying   Klocker
Approximate Cost   ÖS 25,000,000
Site Area   3,877 m²
Building Area   913 m²
Total Floor Area   2,486 m²
Photographer   Eduard Hueber, New York, USA
Further Reading   Domus, October/1995

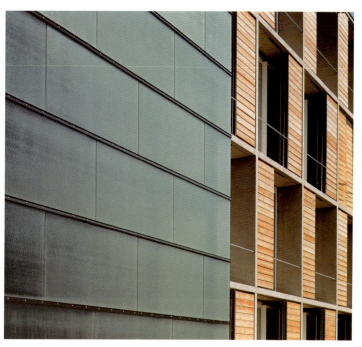

Becker Gewers Kühn & Kühn Architekten, Berlin
Headquarters Verbundnetz Gas AG

Leipzig, Germany
1992–1997

Award   BDA Deubau Preis 1998
Given by   BDA Bund Deutscher Architekten
Prize Presentation   January 1998
Members of the Jury   Lothar Juckel, Annette Jäger, Andres G. Hempel,
    Frank Assmann, Holger Pluder, Richard H. Bause, Jürgen Fissler,
    Hans-Martin Schutte, Hans-Eckhard Lindemann, Irene Wiese von Ofen,
    Oliver Scheytt, Torben Nordstrøm, Alfons Jochems
Structural Engineering   ARUP GmbH, Berlin
Mechanical and Electrical Engineering   J. Roger Preston & Partners, London;
    Klimasystemtechnik, Berlin
Acoustic Engineering   ARUP Acoustics, Winchester, United Kingdom
Façade Consultant   JASP Steinmetz GmbH, Nidda
Lighting Consultant   George Sexton Associates, Washington, DC, USA
Life Safety Consultant   BULL-Ingenieurplan, Waldbronn
Information and Communication Technology   RZ-Plan GmbH, Waldbronn
Art Design   Achenbach Art Consulting, Düsseldorf; James Turrell, Flagstaff,
    Arizona, USA
Landscape Architecture   WES & Partner, Hamburg; Rheims + Partner, Krefeld
Fir Prevention   Hosser, Hass & Partner, Berlin
Cost and Time Controlling   Weiss & Partner, Oberursel
Site Management   Sieme & Geffe Bauplanung, Berlin
Approximate Cost   DM 115,000,000
Site Area   34,529 m²
Building Area   9,136 m²
Total Floor Area   31,826 m²
Photographer   Jens Willebrand, Cologne
Further Reading   Becker Gewers Kühn & Kühn
    Architekten Berlin, Verlag H.M. Nelte

Heinrich Böll, Hans Krabel, Essen
Former Mining Zollverein Schacht XII, Essen

Essen, Germany
1991–1998

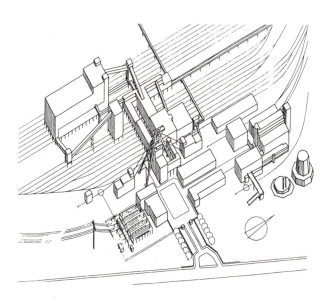

Award   Constructec-Preis 1998
Given by   Deutsche Messe AG with BDA Bund Deutscher Architekten
Prize Presentation   April/21/1998
Members of the Jury   Françoise Hélène Jourda, Jürgen Bredow, Klaus Daniels, Dieter Eberle, Ingeborg Flagge, Nicola Fortmann-Drühe, Karl Ganser, Theo Hotz, Helmut C. Schulitz, Werner Schumann
Design Team   Claudia Blanc, Michael Feisthauer, Claus Filtmann, Stefan Hustadt, Britta Lindemann, Holger Nothnagel, Uwe Schall, Niels Schön, Sven Seidensticker, Josip Topalovic, Wojciech Trompeta, Jolanta Trompeta, Michael Tsitotas, Knut van der Minde, Richard Berger, Heidi Dahlmann, Andreas von Rüden, Dieter Dreßler, Uwe Morsbach, Christel Berger, Elina Kanerva, Petra Tofote
Structural Engineering   W.H.S. Weber – Hamelmann – Surmann, Essen
Civil Engineering   Planergruppe Oberhausen GmbH, Oberhausen
Mechanical Engineering   Stredich + Partner, Mülheim
Electrical Engineering   Stredich + Partner, Mülheim
Environmental Engineering   Planergruppe Oberhausen GmbH, Oberhausen
Acoustic Engineering   Institut für Bauphysik Horst Grün, Mülheim
Air Conditioning Consultant   Ingenieurbüro G. Hoffmann, Essen
Lighting Consultant   Stredich + Partner, Mülheim
Life Safety Consultant   Feuerwehr Stadt Essen
Interior Design   Heinrich Böll; Foster & Partners (Halle 7)
Landscape Architecture   Planergruppe Oberhausen GmbH, Oberhausen
Quantity Surveying   Bauhütte Zeche Zollverein GmbH, Essen
Approximate Cost   DM 88,000,000
Site Area   258,730 m²
Building Area   11,200 m²
Total Floor Area   23,500 m²
Photographer   Susanne Brügger, Jochen Helle, Stephan Pegels
Further Reading   Detail June 1997, pp. 873 ff.

Braun & Voigt und Partner, Frankfurt am Main
MG Office Building, Duisburg-Innenhafen

Duisburg, Germany
October 1992–October 1995

Award   BDA Auszeichnung guter Bauten 1997 der BDA-Kreisgruppe
Rechter Niederrhein (Anerkennung)
Given by   BDA Bund Deutscher Architekten Nordrhein-Westfalen
(Kreisgruppe Rechter Niederrhein)
Prize Presentation   September/20/1996
Members of the Jury   Nikola Fortmann-Drühe, Elmar Schossig, Walter von Lom,
Thomas Finkemeier, Helmut Sachweh, Dressler, Ruppien
Design Team   Braun & Voigt und Partner – Leszek Bylica (Project Leader),
Esther Stäter, Norbert Marx
Structural Engineering   BGS Ingenieursozietät, Beck-Gravert-Schneider,
Frankfurt am Main
Technical Facilities   HK Ingenieurbüro Klöffel VDI, Bruchköbel
Interior Design   Braun & Voigt und Partner
Landscape Architecture   Braun & Voigt und Partner
Quantity Surveying   Ingenieurbüro Brockmann, Frankfurt am Main
Approximate Cost   DM 25,000,000
Site Area   2,200 m²
Building Area   1,600 m²
Total Floor Area   14,000 m²
Photographer   Ralph Richter, Dortmund
Further Reading   Alt und Neu – Tatort Duisburg, In: Bauwelt 3/1996;
Ausgangslage: Sonderfall – Kontorhaus, In: AIT 10/1997

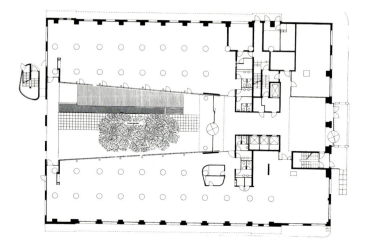

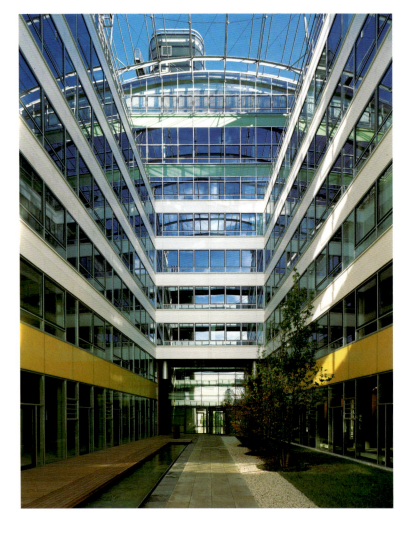

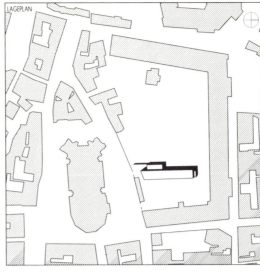

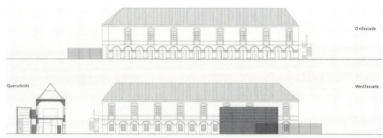

Diözesanbauamt – Karl Frey + Mitarbeiter, Eichstätt
Extension and Conversion of the Orbansaal

Ingolstadt, Germany
1994–1996

Award   Anerkennung BDA Preis Bayern 1997
Given by   BDA Bund Deutscher Architekten Bayern
Prize Presentation   February/3/1998
Members of the Jury   Eric Adlercreutz, Jan Gezelius,
    Peter Kulka, Gerhard Matzig, Gerhard Spangenberg
Design Team   Richard Breitenhuber, Christina Brandl,
    Roland Seidl, Bernhard Fürnrieder
Structural Engineering   Helmut und Klaus Stich, Ingolstadt
Civil Engineering   Grad Ingenieurplanungen, Ingolstadt
Electrical Engineering   Ingenieurbüro Walter Bamberger, Pfünz
Acoustic Engineering   Müller BBM, Planegg
Interior Design   Diözesanbauamt Eichstätt – Karl Frey
Landscape Architecture   Teusch und Partner, Munich
Quantity Surveying   Diözesanbauamt Eichstätt
Approximate Cost   DM 4,500,000
Building Area   543.67 m²
Total Floor Area   735.34 m²
Photographer   Carl Lang, Werner Prokschi

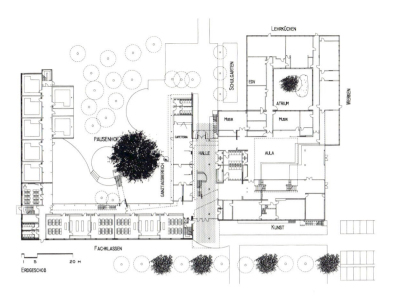

Dohle + Lohse, Brunswick
Extension and Conversion of the Friedensschule School Center Lingen-Darme
Lingen, Germany
1994–1996

Award   BDA Preis Niedersachsen 1997
Given by   BDA Bund Deutscher Architekten Niedersachsen
Prize Presentation   December 1997
Members of the Jury   Paulhans Peters, Anett-Maud Joppien,
   Erhard Tränkner, Thomas van den Valentyn, Bernd Krämer
Design Team   Dohle + Lohse
Structural Engineering   Ingenieurbüro H. Fiedler, Lingen
Mechanical Engineering   HLS R. Beushausen, Lingen
Electrical Engineering   Ingenieurbüro Tautorat, Lingen
Acoustic Engineering   Kötter Beratende Ingenieure, Rheine
Landscape Architecture   Dohle + Lohse with K. Strothmann, Lingen
Approximate Cost   DM 11,000,000
Site Area   21,000 m²
Building Area   1,500 m² (Neubau); 2,850 m² (Altbau)
Total Floor Area   2,900 m² (Neubau); 4,100 m² (Altbau)
Photographer   Klemens Ortmeyer, Brunswick
Further Reading   Architekten in Niedersachsen

Foster and Partners, London, United Kingdom
Microelectronic Center

Duisburg, Germany
1988–1996

Award   BDA Auszeichnung guter Bauten 1997 der BDA-Kreisgruppe Rechter
   Niederrhein (Auszeichnung)
Given by   BDA Bund Deutscher Architekten Nordrhein-Westfalen (Kreisgruppe
   Rechter Niederrhein)
Prize Presentation   September/20/1996
Members of the Jury   Nikola Fortmann-Drühe, Elmar Schossig, Walter von Lom,
   Thomas Finkemeier, Helmut Sachweh, Dressler, Ruppien
Architects and Landscape Designers   Foster and Partners, London, United Kingdom
Project Manager and Cost Control   Diederichs & Partner, Wuppertal
Site Supervision & Specification   Höhler & Partner, Aachen
Structural Engineering   Reinhold Meyer, Kassel
Mechanical Engineering   Ebert Ingenieure, Nuremberg; Kaiser Bautechnik, Duisburg
Electrical Engineering   Ebert Ingenieure, Nuremberg; Kaiser Bautechnik, Duisburg
Cladding Consultant   Emmer Pfenninger Partner AG, Münchenstein, Switzerland
Fire Consultant   Klingsch, Wuppertal
Acoustic Engineering   ITA GmbH, Wiesbaden
Landscape Architecture   Benning, Münster
Quantity Surveying   Dierk Dördelmann, Duisburg
Soil Consultant   Harries Pickel Consult, Duisburg
Approximate Cost   DM 33,000,000
Site Area   15,000 m^2
Building Area   12,000 m^2
Photographer   Nigel Young
Further Reading   The Architect's Journal, July/3/1997

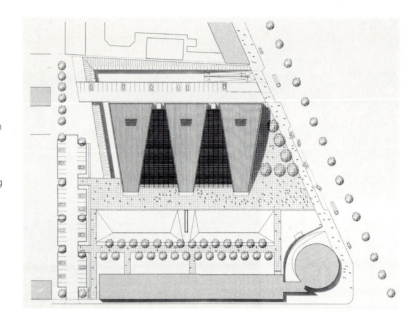

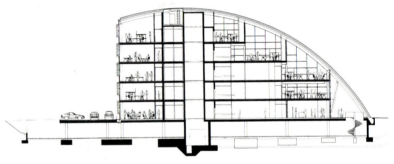

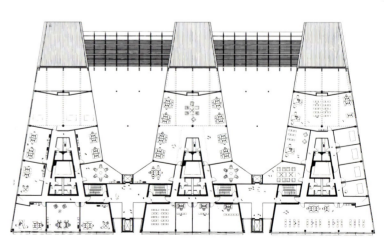

Friedrich und Partner, Düsseldorf
Headquarters of the Stadtwerke Witten
Witten, Germany
1989–1995

Award   BDA Auszeichnung guter Bauten 1997 der BDA-Kreisgruppe Bochum
Given by   BDA Bund Deutscher Architekten Nordrhein-Westfalen
   (Kreisgruppe Bochum)
Prize Presentation   November/15/1997
Members of the Jury   Jean Flammang, Zamp Kelp, Klaus Köpke,
   Joachim König, Christian Schaller, Hans-Günter Golinski
Design Team   Detlev Korn, Götz Schneider, Elmar Rottkamp, Elke Banz,
   Christina Dirk, Jörg Friedrich, Anna Holmwood, Wilfried Kneffel, Ralf Kohfeld,
   Andreas Kühn, Kirsten Sommer, Nadja Trageser, Lars Wittorf, Carlo Zilli
Structural Engineering   Ingenieurgesellschaft für Baukonstruktion
   Horz + Ladewig, Cologne
Mechanical Engineering   Riedel, Holzwickede
Electrical Engineering   Ingenieurbüro für Elektroplanung Kubitza VDE, LITG,
   Recklinghausen
Acoustic Engineering   Trümper, Overrath, Heimann & Römer, Bergisch-Gladbach
Lighting Consultant   Erco Leuchten, Lüdenscheidt
Interior Design   Friedrich + Partner, Hamburg/Düsseldorf
Landscape Architecture   Friedrich + Partner, Hamburg/Düsseldorf
Approximate Cost   DM 35,000,000
Total Floor Area   30,000 m²
Photographer   Klaus Frahm, Börnsen – Hamburg
Further Reading   Friedrich, Jörg: Hauptverwaltung der Stadtwerke Witten,
   hg. von Ingeborg Flagge, 1994

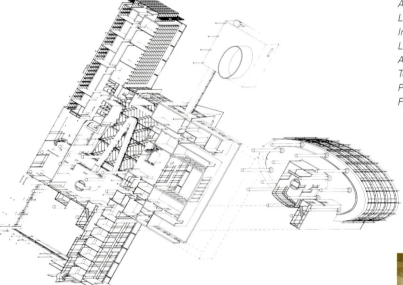

Gruhl & Partner, Cologne
Schäfer House, Meerbusch-Brüderich

Ahornstraße, Düsseldorf, Germany
1991–1993

Award   BDA Auszeichnung guter Bauten 1997
   der BDA-Kreisgruppe Düsseldorf
Given by   BDA Bund Deutscher Architekten Nordrhein-Westfalen
   (Kreisgruppe Düsseldorf)
Prize Presentation   September/23/1997
Members of the Jury   Heinrich Böll, Johannes Busmann,
   Ulrich Erben, Hans Hoorn, Walter von Lom, Manfred Morlock,
   Wolfgang Pehnt, G.C. Wagner
Design Team   Gruhl & Partner – Hartmut Gruhl,
   Ursula Gonsior, Sabine Hersch
Structural Engineering   Gerhard Spiessbach
Mechanical Engineering   Hans-Georg Schäfer
Electrical Engineering   Hans-Georg Schäfer
Interior Design   Gruhl & Partner
Landscape Architecture   Bernhard Korte
Approximate Cost   DM 2,500,000
Site Area   2,800 m²
Building Area   176 m²
Total Floor Area   450 m²
Photographer   Hajo Willig, Marion Nickig

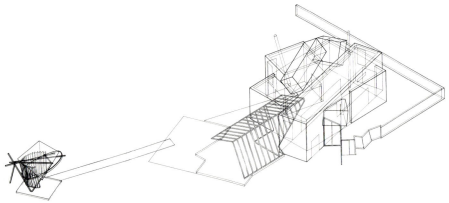

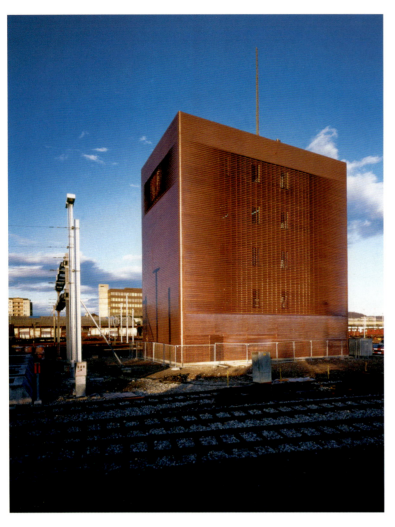

Herzog & de Meuron, Basle
SBB Switch Tower 4, Auf dem Wolf

Basle, Switzerland
1989–1994

Award Constructec-Preis 1996 (Special Award)
Given by Deutsche Messe AG with BDA Bund Deutscher Architekten
Prize Presentation June/19/1996
Members of the Jury Thomas Herzog, Mels Crouwel, Klaus Daniels, Dörte
  Gatermann, Jesper Gottlieb, Sepp D. Heckmann, Andreas Gottlieb Hempel,
  Bernd Steigerwald, Frank Werner
Partners in Charge Jacques Herzog, Pierre de Meuron, Harry Gugger (Project
  Architect), Hansueli Suter, Klaus Loehnert, Philippe Fürstenberger (Collaborators)
Structural Engineering Proplan Ing. AG, Basle
Construction Management Proplan Ing. AG, Basle
Electrical Planning Selmoni AG, Basle
General Planning Proplan Ing. AG (Project Leader: A. Vorraro), Basle
Special Planning Fassade Tecton AG, Basle
Climate Control Design Sulzer Energieconsulting AG, Liestal
Sanitary Planning Balduin Weisser AG, Basle
Approximate Cost SFR 6,170,000
Building Area 286 m²
Total Floor Area 1,893 m²
Photographer Margherita Spiluttini, Hisao Suzuki (model)

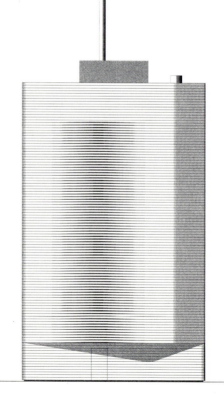

Theo Hotz, Zurich
Operational Facilities for the Gasworks – Public Utilities
Winterthur, Switzerland
February 1990–March 1996

Award   Constructec-Preis 1996
Given by   Deutsche Messe AG with BDA Bund Deutscher Architekten
Prize Presentation   June/19/1996
Members of the Jury   Thomas Herzog, Mels Crouwel,
    Klaus Daniels, Dörte Gatermann, Jesper Gottlieb, Sepp D. Heckmann,
    Andreas Gottlieb Hempel, Bernd Steigerwald, Frank Werner
Structural Engineering   Werner Höhn, Winterthur
Mechanical Engineering   Meier + Wirz AG, Winterthur
Electrical Engineering   Städtische Werke; Installation Elektrizität Winterthur
Quantity Surveying   Theo Hotz AG
Approximate Cost   SFR 55,000,000
Site Area   13,000 m²
Building Area   5,200 m²
Total Floor Area   8,700 m²
Photographer   Markus Fischer, Zurich
Further Reading   Bauwelt 43/44,
    November/22/1996, p. 2494

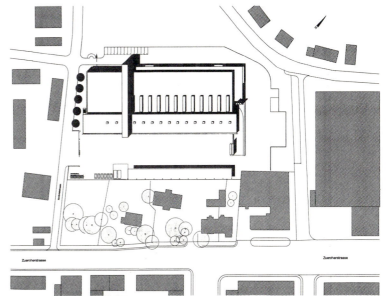

Ingenhoven Overdiek Kahlen + Partner, Düsseldorf
Kaistrasse 16a, Offices and Studios
Düsseldorf, Germany
December 1994–July 1997

Award   BDA Auszeichnung guter Bauten 1997
  der BDA-Kreisgruppe Düsseldorf
Given by   BDA Bund Deutscher Architekten Nordrhein-Westfalen
  (Kreisgruppe Düsseldorf)
Prize Presentation   September/23/1997
Members of the Jury   Heinrich Böll, Johannes Busmann, Ulrich Erben,
  Hans Hoorn, Walter von Lom, Manfred Morlock, Wolfgang Pehnt, G.C. Wagner
Design Team   Ingenhoven Overdiek Kahlen + Partner – Christoph Debiel
  (Project Leader), Ralf Dorsch-Rüter, Raoul Schwarz, Ralf Walter, Martina Pesch
  (Collaborators)
Structural Engineering   ARUP GmbH, Düsseldorf
Mechanical Engineering   Wolfferts GmbH, Essen
Electrical Engineering   Elan GmbH, Remscheid
Acoustic Engineering   D + S – Plan, Cologne
Air Conditioning Consultant   Wolfferts GmbH, Essen
Lighting Consultant   HL-Technik, Munich
Approximate Cost   DM 24,300,000
Site Area   800 m^2
Building Area   800 m^2
Total Floor Area   4,785 m^2

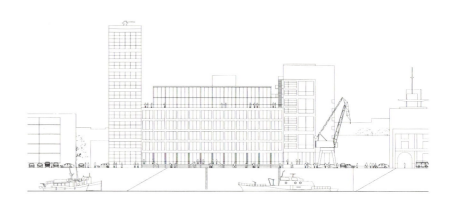

Jauss + Gaupp, Friedrichshafen
Zeppelinmuseum
Friedrichshafen, Germany
1991–1996

Award   Hugo-Häring-Preis 1997 des BDA Baden-Württemberg
Given by   BDA Bund Deutscher Architekten Baden-Württemberg
Prize Presentation   October/14/1997
Members of the Jury   Karl Baumschlager, Gerhart Laage, Eberhardt Palmer, Matthias Sauerbruch, Michael Schumacher, Rudolf Stegers
Design Team   Markus Klein (Project Architect), Uwe Blasberg, Hansjörg Obergfell, Christine Köhle, Rainer Girke, Elke Linse, Bernd Haug, Johann Veeser, Hans-Peter Holzer, Ulrich Kluth, Stefan Amann, Michael Zwölfer
Structural Engineering   Leonhardt, Andrä + Partner, Stuttgart
Mechanical Engineering   Rentschler + Riedesser, Stuttgart
Electrical Engineering   Schlaefle, Konstanz
Acoustic Engineering   ITA GmbH, Wiesbaden-Delkenheim
Air Conditioning Consultant   Rentschler + Riedesser, Stuttgart
Lighting Consultant   Schlaefle, Konstanz
Landscape Architecture   Jauss + Gaupp, Friedrichshafen
Quantity Surveying   Jauss + Gaupp, Friedrichshafen
Approximate Cost   DM 76,000,000
Building Area   3,010 m²
Total Floor Area   11,599 m²
Photographer   Myrzik + Jarisch, Munich
Further Reading   Bauwelt 9/1996

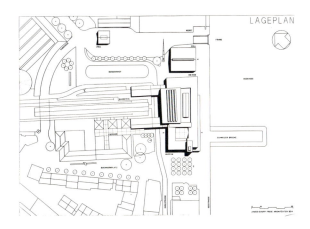

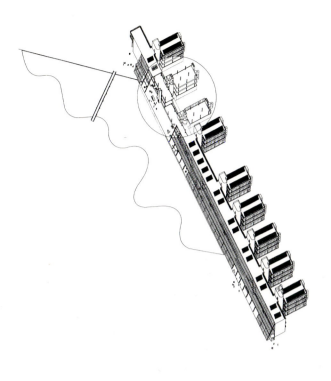

Kiessler + Partner, Munich
Science Park Gelsenkirchen

Gelsenkirchen, Germany
1989–1995

Award   Constructec-Preis 1998 (Special Award)
Given by   Deutsche Messe AG with BDA Bund Deutscher Architekten
Prize Presentation   April/21/1998
Members of the Jury   Françoise Hélène Jourda, Jürgen Bredow, Klaus Daniels,
  Dieter Eberle, Ingeborg Flagge, Nicola Fortmann-Drühe, Karl Ganser, Theo Hotz,
  Helmut C. Schulitz, Werner Schumann
Design Team   Kiessler + Partner
Structural Engineering   Sailer + Stepan, Munich
Electrical Engineering   Riemhofer/Zerull, Munich
Environmental Engineering   Ingenieurbüro Trumpp, Gräfelfing
Acoustic Engineering   Müller BBM, Munich
Air Conditioning Consultant   Ingenieurbüro Trumpp, Gräfelfing
Landscape Architecture   Planungsbüro Drecker, Bottrop-Kirchhellen
Quantity Surveying   Suter + Suter, Düsseldorf
Approximate Cost   DM 70,000,000
Total Floor Area   27,200 m²
Photographer   Ralph Richter, Düsseldorf, Lukas Roth, Ulf Stein
Further Reading   Bauwelt 9/1995

Kai-Michael Koch, Anne Panse, Andreas-Christian Kühn, Hanover
Kestner Gesellschaft Hanover, Conversion of the former Goseriede Baths into an Art Gallery

Hanover, Germany
1994–1997

Award BDA Preis Niedersachsen 1997
Given by BDA Bund Deutscher Architekten Niedersachsen
Prize Presentation December 1997
Members of the Jury Paulhans Peters, Anett-Maud Joppien,
  Erhard Tränkner, Thomas van den Valentyn, Bernd Krämer
Structural Engineering Ingenieurbüro Kreutzfeld, Hanover
Electrical Engineering EBH Elektrobau Hanover
Acoustic Engineering Ingenieurbüro Wietfeldt, Burgdorf
Air Conditioning Consultant Passau Ingenieure GmbH, Düsseldorf
Lighting Consultant Licht-Kunst-Licht GmbH, Bonn/Berlin
Approximate Cost DM 11,500,000
Site Area 1,450 m²
Building Area 1,275 m²
Total Floor Area 2,600 m²
Photographer Peter Gauditz, Hanover

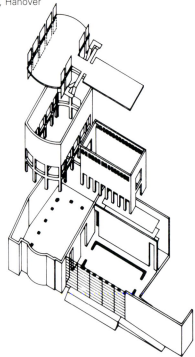

Kohl & Kohl Architekten, Duisburg / Essen
Musical Theater Colosseum

Essen, Germany
1995–1996

Award   Constructec-Preis 1998 (Special Award)
Given by   Deutsche Messe AG with BDA Bund Deutscher Architekten
Prize Presentation   April/21/1998
Members of the Jury   Françoise Hélène Jourda, Jürgen Bredow, Klaus Daniels,
   Dieter Eberle, Ingeborg Flagge, Nicola Fortmann-Drühe, Karl Ganser, Theo Hotz,
   Helmut C. Schulitz, Werner Schumann
Civil Engineering   W.H.S Weber – Hamelmann – Surmann, Essen
Mechanical Engineering   HL-Technik, Düsseldorf
Electrical Engineering   HL-Technik, Düsseldorf
Environmental Engineering   HL-Technik, Düsseldorf
Acoustic Engineering   ITAB, Dortmund
Air Conditioning Consultant   HL-Technik, Düsseldorf
Lighting Consultant   Graham Phoenix, LDP, London
Interior Design   Backstage Cafe, Christoph Stierli, Zurich
Landscape Architecture   Klein, Weber, Maas, Düsseldorf
Quantity Surveying   Kohl & Kohl Architekten
Approximate Cost   DM 50,000,000
Site Area   5,000 m²
Building Area   4,200 m²
Total Floor Area   13,000 m²
Photographer   Jens Willebrandt, Cologne
Further Reading   Bauwelt 3/1996

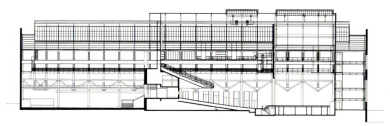

Gerd Lindemann + Florian Thamm, Brunswick
Theater Kleines Haus

Brunswick, Germany
1989–1996

Award   BDA Preis Niedersachsen 1997
Given by   BDA Bund Deutscher Architekten Niedersachsen
Prize Presentation   December 1997
Members of the Jury   Paulhans Peters, Anett-Maud Joppien,
   Erhard Tränkner, Thomas van den Valentyn, Bernd Krämer
Design Team   Gerd Lindemann, Heinz Wilke (Design), Claus Dölling,
   Horst Klocke, Horst Marten, Christine Schütz, Jörg Schulz-Behrendt,
   Beate Broda-Lange, Florian Thamm, Heinrich Steiln (Building Supervision)
Structural Engineering   Hage + Partner, Brunswick
Civil Engineering   GGU Gesellschaft für Umwelttechnik, Brunswick
Mechanical Engineering   Biste + Gerling, Berlin
Electrical Engineering   Biste + Gerling, Berlin
Acoustic Engineering   Benke, Daberto + Partner, Sehnde
Air Conditioning Consultant   Becker + Becker, Brunswick
Lighting Consultant   Conceptlicht, Mils Hall, Austria
Interior Design   Lindemann + Thamm, Brunswick
Landscape Architecture   Wehberg-Eppinger-Schmittke, Hamburg
Approximate Cost   DM 46,000,000
Site Area   1,700 m²
Building Area   1,500 m²
Total Floor Area   5,000 m²
Photographer   Klemens Ortmeyer, Brunswick
Further Reading   CENTRUM, Jahrbuch Architektur und Stadt, 1996

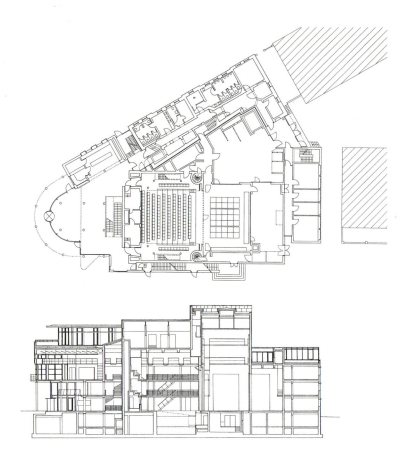

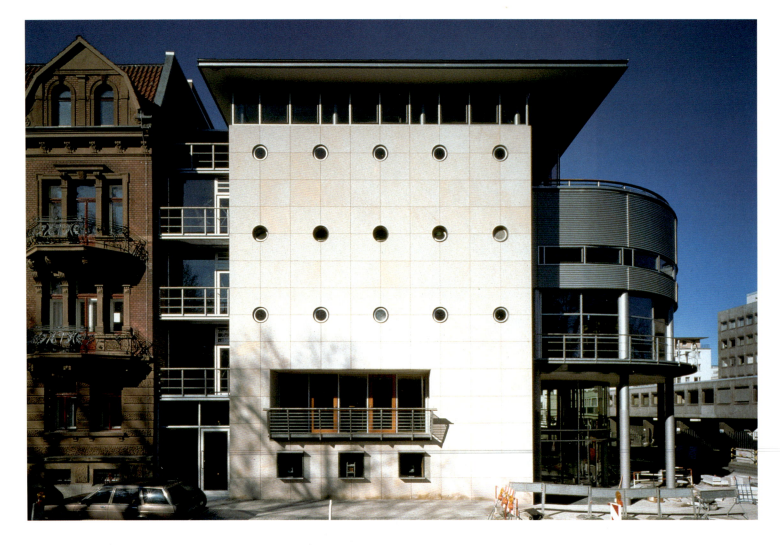

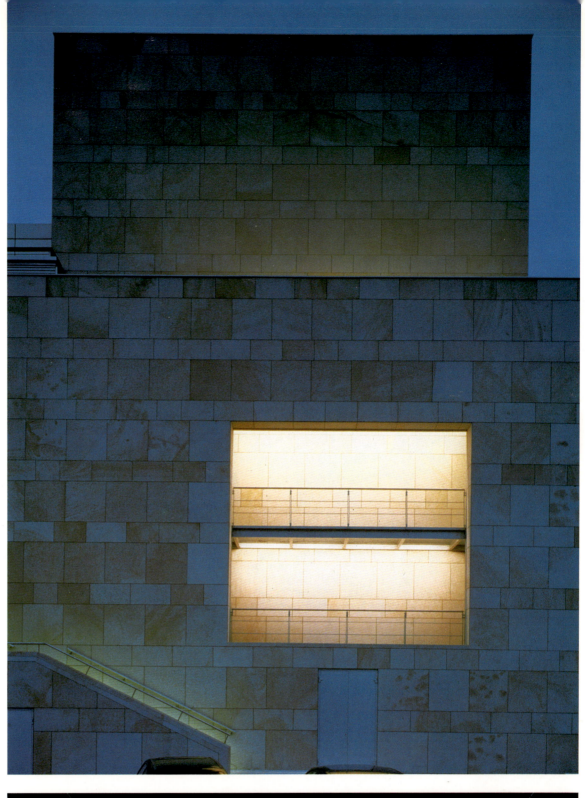

Andreas Ortner, Gabriele Ortner, Graz
Workshop A. & C. Wallner

Scheifling, Austria
1993–1994

Award   Constructec-Preis 1996 (Special Award)
Given by   Deutsche Messe AG with BDA Bund Deutscher Architekten
Prize Presentation   June/19/1996
Members of the Jury   Thomas Herzog, Mels Crouwel, Klaus Daniels, Dörte
   Gatermann, Jesper Gottlieb, Sepp D. Heckmann, Andreas Gottlieb Hempel,
   Bernd Steigerwald, Frank Werner
Design Team   Andreas Ortner, Gabriele Ortner
Structural Engineering   Rüdiger Koberg
Civil Engineering   Andreas Ortner, Gabriele Ortner
Electrical Engineering   Domberger, Elektro Leitner
Acoustic Engineering   Andreas Ortner, Gabriele Ortner
Air Conditioning Consultant   Zeiringer – Spreitzer
Lighting Consultant   Andreas Ortner and Gabriele Ortner
Interior Design   Andreas Ortner, Gabriele Ortner
Landscape Architecture   Gabriele Ortner
Quantity Surveying   Andreas Ortner and Gabriele Ortner
Approximate Cost   ÖS 6,000,000
Site Area   2,040 m²
Building Area   566.50 m²
Total Floor Area   932 m²
Photographer   Peter Eder, Gerald Zugmann, Walter Luttenberger

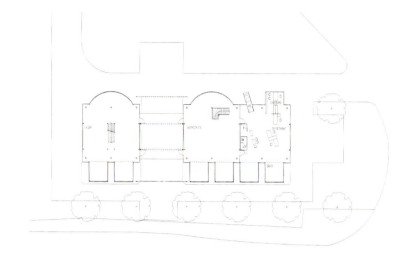

Dominique Perrault, Paris
Water Purification Plant Sagep

Irry-sur-Seine, France
1987–1993

Award   Constructec-Preis 1996 (Special Award)
Given by   Deutsche Messe AG with BDA Bund Deutscher Architekten
Prize Presentation   June/19/1996
Members of the Jury   Thomas Herzog, Mels Crouwel, Klaus Daniels,
  Dörte Gatermann, Jesper Gottlieb, Sepp D. Heckmann, Andreas Gottlieb Hempel,
  Bernd Steigerwald, Frank Werner
Design Team   Dominique Perrault with Hervé Cividino, Philippe Gregoire,
  Aude Perrault, Gaélle Lauriot-Prevost
Engineering   Group OTV – Degrepont Setec – Foulquier
Interior Design   Dominique Perrault with his Design Team
Quantity Surveying   SETEC Ingénièrie
Approximate Cost   FF 500,000,000 (with Technical Equipment)
Site Area   90,000 m² (Offices 1,900 m²)
Photographer   Michel Denancé
Further Reading   Techniques & Architecture, May 1994

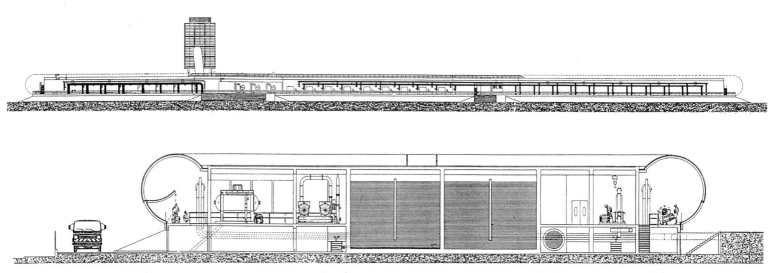

Hartwig N. Schneider, Stuttgart
Kindergarten Lange Weiden
Winnenden, Germany
1994–1995

Award   Hugo-Häring-Preis 1997 des BDA Baden-Württemberg
Given by   BDA Bund Deutscher Architekten Baden-Württemberg
Prize Presentation   October/14/1997
Members of the Jury   Karl Baumschlager, Gerhart Laage,
   Eberhardt Palmer, Matthias Sauerbruch, Michael Schumacher, Rudolf Stegers
Design Team   Hartwig N. Schneider with Gabriele Mayer, Ingo Pelchen,
   Christof Birkel, John Barnbrook
Structural Engineering   Jauss; Sobek und Rieger (Consultants)
Landscape Architecture   Gesswein, Henkel und Partner, Ostfildern
Site Area   1,734 m²
Building Area   445 m²
Total Floor Area   846 m²
Photographer   Christian Kandzia

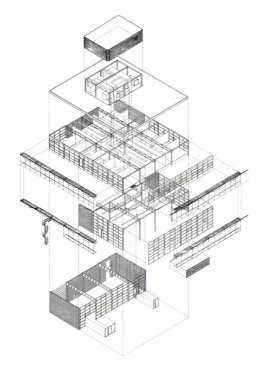

Schulitz + Partner – Helmut C. Schulitz, Stefan Worbes, Brunswick
IAM Institute for Applied Microelectronics

Brunswick, Germany
1992–1994

Award   Constructec-Preis 1996 (Special Award)
Given by   Deutsche Messe AG with BDA Bund Deutscher Architekten
Prize Presentation   June/19/1996
Members of the Jury   Thomas Herzog, Mels Crouwel,
   Klaus Daniels, Dörte Gatermann, Jesper Gottlieb, Sepp D. Heckmann,
   Andreas Gottlieb Hempel, Bernd Steigerwald, Frank Werner
Design Team   Helmut C. Schulitz, Stefan Worbes, Reto J. Aus der Au,
   Michael Asche
Structural Engineering   Harden + Partner, Brunswick
Mechanical Engineering   Riechers, Brunswick
Electrical Engineering   Lindhorst, Brunswick
Air Conditioning Consultant   Riechers, Brunswick
Interior Design   Schulitz + Partner
Landscape Architecture   Roedenbeck, Brunswick
Quantity Surveying   Schulitz + Partner
Approximate Cost   DM 7,500,000
Site Area   7,399 m²
Building Area   653 m²
Total Floor Area   1,838 m²
Photographer   Schulitz + Partner
Further Reading   Schulitz + Partner, Bauten + Projekte,
   In: Architectural Review, Ernst & Sohn Verlag, Berlin

Schuster Architekten, Düsseldorf
School Building, Realschule Voerde

Voerde, Germany
November 1994–Mai 1996

Award   BDA Auszeichnung guter Bauten 1997 der BDA-Kreisgruppe
   Rechter Niederrhein
Given by   BDA Bund Deutscher Architekten Nordrhein-Westfalen
   (Kreisgruppe Rechter Niederrhein)
Prize Presentation   September/20/1996
Members of the Jury   Nikola Fortmann-Drühe, Elmar Schossig,
   Walter von Lom, Thomas Finkemeier, Helmut Sachweh, Dressler, Ruppien
Structural Engineering   Büro Stracke, Cologne
Civil Engineering   Büro Bayer, Düsseldorf
Electrical Engineering   Büro Quel, Wuppertal
Acoustic Engineering   Büro Zeller + Partner, Essen
Approximate Cost   DM 6,100,000
Building Area   1,705 m^2
Photographer   Frank Springer, Düsseldorf
Further Reading   Bauwelt 28/1996; Detail 4/1997

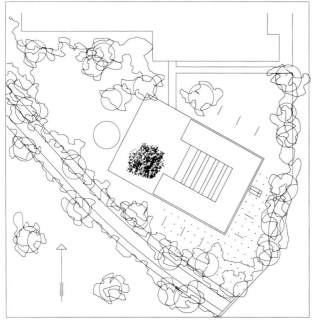

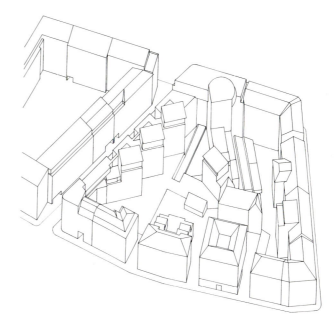

Steidle + Partner, Munich
Wacker-Haus, Office and Residential Building of the Pensionskasse der Wacker-Chemie
Prinzregentenstraße, Munich, Germany
1992–1997

Award   Deutscher Städtebaupreis
Given by   BDA Bund Deutscher Architekten
Prize Presentation   December/1/1997
Members of the Jury   Ulrich Conrads, Barbara Fleckenstein, Jürgen Hanne,
   Ulrich Kerkhoff, Antje Kossak, Gisela Kraft
Design Team   Otto Steidle, Hans Kohl, Erich Gassmann
Collaborators   Martin Klein, Begoña Gonzalo Orden, Claudia Dias, Martina Hornhardt
Engineering   Obermeyer Planen + Bauen, Munich – Jochen Lüdecke
   (Project Manager), Konrad Zacherl (Structural Engineering), Bartlin Brauchle
   (Civil Engineering)
Site Management   Christina Högerl – Steidle und Partner; Stefan Pfundstein,
   Udo Raab, Josef Weidinger – Obermeyer Planen + Bauen
Lighting Consultant   Werner Lampel, Diessen
Landscape Architecture   Latz + Partner, Ampertshausen; Muhammad Abdullah
   Mumme (Garden Art), Munich
Quantity Surveying   ALBA Allgemeine Bau- und Anlagen-Planungsgesellschaft mbH,
   Grünwald
Approximate Cost   DM 70,000,000
Total Floor Area   16,000 m²
Photographer   Stefan Müller-Naumann

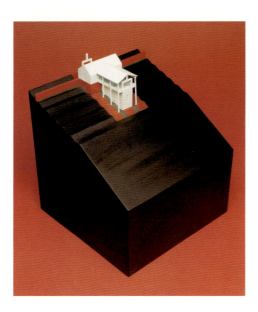

Peter Stürzebecher, Hamburg/Berlin
T-House
Gleisweiler, Germany
1989–1990

Award   BDA Preis Rheinland-Pfalz 1997
Given by   BDA Bund Deutscher Architekten Rheinland-Pfalz
Prize Presentation   June/15/1997
Members of the Jury   Jürgen Bredow, Gernot Kramer,
    Norbert Zenner, Bernd Goldmann
Structural Engineering   Natterer + Dittrich
Landscape Architecture   Peter Stürzebecher
Approximate Cost   DM 447,000
Site Area   2,500 m^2
Building Area   99 m^2
Total Floor Area   229.74 m^2
Photographer   Rainer Stocké, Frankenthal
Further Reading   Bauwelt; Technique Architecture

Hans-Busso von Busse, Eberhard C. Klapp, Essen
Witten House
Witten, Germany
1990–1996

Award   1) Grand Prix Rhénan d' Architecture 1997 (1ère mention);
    2) BDA Auszeichnung guter Bauten 1997 der BDA-Kreisgruppe Bochum
Given by   1) BDA Bund Deutscher Architekten Rheinland-Pfalz, BNA Bond van
    Nederlandse Architekten, Conseil National de l'Ordre des Architectes, BSA;
    2) BDA Bund Deutscher Architekten Nordrhein-Westfalen (Kreisgruppe Bochum)
Prize Presentation   1) July/10/1997; 2) November/15/1997
Members of the Jury   Katharina Knapkiewics, Pierre Bonnet, At Tunis,
    Meindert Booy, Jochem Jourdan, Bruno Decaris; 2) Jean Flammang,
    Zamp Kelp, Klaus Köpke, Joachim König, Christian Schaller, Hans-Günter Golinski
Design Team   Hans-Busso von Busse, Eberhard C. Klapp, Arndt Brüning,
    Andrea Eggenmüller, Volker Rein
Structural Engineering   Ingenieurbüro Meyer, Bochum
Civil Engineering   Ingeniuerbüro Meyer, Bochum
Electrical Engineering   Stadt Witten
Acoustic Engineering   Ingenieurbüro Peutz, Düsseldorf
Air Conditioning Consultant   Ingenieurbüro Kahlert, Haltern
Lighting Consultant   ERCO Lüdenscheid
Interior Design   Hans-Busso von Busse, Eberhard C. Klapp
Landscape Architecture   Hans-Busso von Busse, Eberhard C. Klapp
Quantity Surveying   Hans-Busso von Busse, Eberhard C. Klapp
Approximate Cost   DM 18,000,000
Building Area   2,840 m²
Photographer   Winde Fotodesign, Bochum

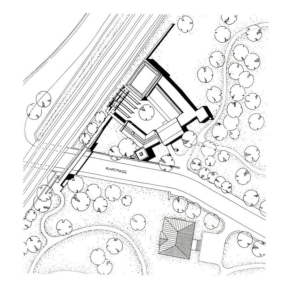

Architekten von Gerkan, Marg & Partner, Hamburg
Galeria Duisburg

Duisburg, Germany
1989–1994

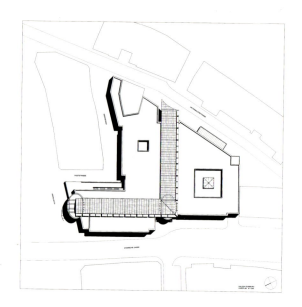

Award   BDA Auszeichnung guter Bauten 1997 der BDA-Kreisgruppe
   Rechter Niederrhein (Anerkennung)
Given by   BDA Bund Deutscher Architekten Nordrhein-Westfalen
   (Kreisgruppe Rechter Niederrhein)
Prize Presentation   September/20/1996
Members of the Jury   Nikola Fortmann-Drühe, Elmar Schossig,
   Walter von Lom, Thomas Finkemeier, Helmut Sachweh, Dressler, Ruppien
Design Team   Meinhard von Gerkan with Klaus Staratzke, Otto Dorn
Structural Engineering   Lewenton, Werner, Schwarz, Duisburg
Civil Engineering   Højgaard + Schultz GmbH, Denmark
Mechanical Engineering   Højgaard + Schultz GmbH, Denmark
Electrical Engineering   Højgaard + Schultz GmbH, Denmark
Environmental Engineering   Højgaard + Schultz GmbH, Denmark
Acoustic Engineering   DS – Plan, Cologne
Air Conditioning Consultant   Hojgaard + Schultz GmbH, Denmark
Lighting Consultant   Bartenbach, Innsbruck
Approximate Cost   DM 85,000,000
Site Area   Cubic Content 150,000 m3
Building Area   Cubic Content 150,000 m3
Total Floor Area   32,000 m²
Photographer   Klaus Frahm
Further Reading   von Gerkan, Marg und Partner,
   Architecture 1991–1995

Zach + Zünd Architekten – Gundula Zach, Michel Zünd, Zurich / Stuttgart
Haus Götz, Commercial Building at the Lake

Böblingen, Germany
January 1993 – March 1996

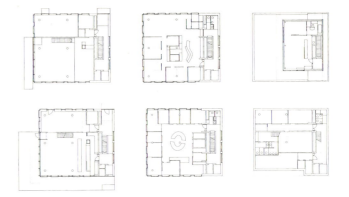

Award   Hugo-Häring-Preis 1997 des BDA Baden-Württemberg
Given by   BDA Bund Deutscher Architekten Baden-Württemberg
Prize Presentation   October/14/1997
Members of the Jury   Karl Baumschlager, Gerhart Laage, Eberhardt Palmer,
    Matthias Sauerbruch, Michael Schumacher, Rudolf Stegers
Design Team   Gundula Zach, Michael Zünd, Fridolin Wetli
Static Engineering   Fischer und Friedrich, Stuttgart
Electrical Engineering   Ingenieurgesellschaft Wetzstein, Herrenberg
Air Conditioning, Heating, Airing, Sanitation Consultant   Ingenieurbüro Schreiber, Ulm
Interior Design   Zach + Zünd Architekten
Landscape Architecture   Zach + Zünd Architekten
Quantity Surveying   Zach + Zünd Architekten
Approximate Cost   DM 4,000,000
Building Area   255 m²
Total Floor Area   978 m²
Photographer   Heinrich Helfenstein, Zurich
Further Reading   Architektur Aktuell, Wien 1995/1996

Günter Zamp Kelp and Julius Krauss, Arno Brandlhuber, Düsseldorf
Neanderthal Museum

Mettmann, Germany
August 1993–October 1996

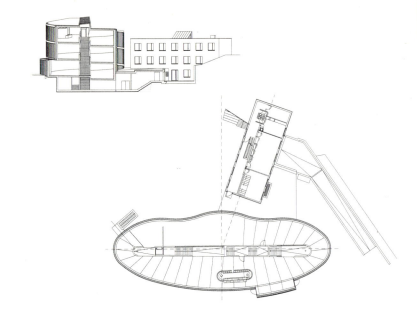

Award   BDA Auszeichnung guter Bauten 1997 der BDA-Kreisgruppe Düsseldorf
Given by   BDA Bund Deutscher Architekten Nordrhein-Westfalen
   (Kreisgruppe Düsseldorf)
Prize Presentation   September/23/1997
Members of the Jury   Heinrich Böll, Johannes Busmann, Ulrich Erben,
   Hans Hoorn, Walter von Lom, Manfred Morlock, Wolfgang Pehnt, G.C. Wagner
Design Team   Thomas Gutt (Project Leader), Astrid Becker, Marco Glashagen,
   Carlos Martin Gonzalez, Götz Leimkühler, Alexei Kouzmine
Structural Engineering   Hochtief AG, Essen
Civil Engineering   Hochtief AG, Düsseldorf
Electrical Engineering   Siemens AG, Düsseldorf
Environmental Engineering   R. Dorff, Bonn
Acoustic Engineering   R. Dorff, Bonn
Air Conditioning Consultant   Bahlmann und Partner, Mettmann
Lighting Consultant   Erco Leuchten GmbH, Lüdenscheid
Life Safety Consultant   Kohlen, Mettmann
Interior Design   Creamuse, Strasbourg
Landscape Architecture   Günter Zamp Kelp and Julius Krauss,
   Arno Brandlhuber
Quantity Surveying   Pelége (Allemagne), Ratingen
Approximate Cost   DM 8,750,000
Site Area   7,246 m^2
Building Area   1,180 m^2
Total Floor Area   3,534.79 m^2
Photographer   Michael Reisch, Düsseldorf
Further Reading   DAM Architektur Jahrbuch 1997, Prestel Verlag
   Munich/New York, pp.136–141; SD 9710 Tokyo; DOMUS 789/1997

P & T Architects and Engineers Ltd., Hong Kong
City Tower

Hong Kong
1995–1997

Award   Certificate of Merit 1997
Given by   HKIA The Hong Kong Institute of Architects
Prize Presentation   February/27/1998
Members of the Jury   Gary Chang, Keith Griffiths, Joseph Ho,
   Lam Wo Hei, Bowen Leung
Design Team   Bing Kwan, William Yuen, Janette Chan, Zenith Chan
Structural Engineering   P & T Architects and Engineers Ltd., Hong Kong
Mechanical Engineering   P & T (M&E) Architects and Engineers Ltd., Hong Kong
Lighting Consultant   Linbeck Rausch Ltd.
Interior Design   P & T Architects and Engineers Ltd., Hong Kong
Quantity Surveying   Bridgewater & Coulton Ltd.
Approximate Cost   US$ 6,500,000
Site Area   289 m²
Building Area   4,335 m²
Photographer   Bobby Sum
Further Reading   A/U Interior, Architecture and Urbanism

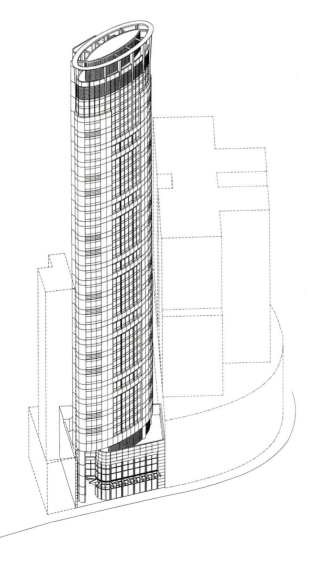

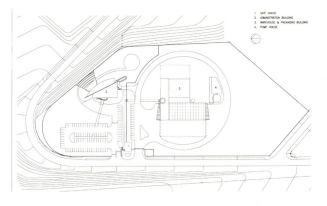

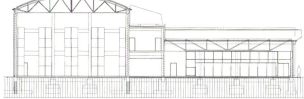

László Szász, Erzsébet Hajnády, Pécs
Glaxo Wellcome Headquarters and
Warehouse – Packaging Building

Törökbálint, Hungary
May 1994–September 1996

Award   Pro Architectura Prize
Given by   Association of Hungarian Architects
Prize Presentation   July/1/1997
Members of the Jury   Péter Szaló, Imre Kovács, Imre Körmendi,
  Gábor Winkler, Pál Nagy, János Gömöri, Csaba Masznyik
Structural Engineering   Katalin Lendvai
Civil Engineering   Lászlo Sándi
Mechanical Engineering   Otto Pfenningberger
Electrical Engineering   István Papp, Péter Komm
Acoustic Engineering   András Kotsy
Life Safety Consultant   Zoltán Papp
Interior Design   Zoltaán Horváth
Landscape Architecture   Sarolta Torma
Quantity Surveying   Gábor Lipcsei
Approximate Cost   HUF 4,400,000
Site Area   30,146 m²
Building Area   2,560 m²
Total Floor Area   5,560 m²
Photographer   Andrea Häider
Further Reading   ÁTRIUM Magazin, 1998/1

O'Donnell & Tuomey, Dublin
Blackwood Golf Centre

Near Bangor, Co. Down, Northern Ireland
1992–1994

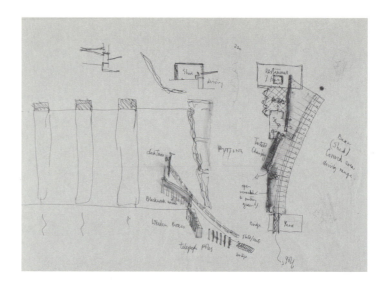

Award   RIAI Triennial Gold Medal 1992–1993–1994 (Commended)
Given by   RIAI The Royal Institute of Architects of Ireland
Prize Presentation   March 1998
Members of the Jury   Sean O'Laoire, Deirdre O'Connor, Joe Kennedy
Design Team   Sheila O'Donnell, John Tuomey, Will Dimond
Structural Engineering   Armstrong + Shaw
Mechanical Engineering   Buckley + Downie
Electrical Engineering   Buckley + Downie
Quantity Surveying   Bruce Shaw Partnership, Dublin/Belfast
Approximate Cost   £ 1,300,000
Site Area   9,000 m²
Building Area   3,600 m²
Total Floor Area   800 m²
Photographer   Christopher Hill
Further Reading   Domus 781/April 1996

Shigeru Ban, Tokyo
Paper Church

Takatori, Hyogo, Japan
March 1995–September 1995

Award   JIA Prize for the Best Young Architect of the Year 1997
Given by   JIA The Japan Institute of Architects
Prize Presentation   September/22/1997
Members of the Jury   Koichi Nagashima, Waro Kishi, Norihiko Dan
Structural Engineering   Gengo Matsui, Shuichi Hoshino
General Contractors   Volonters
Building Area   168.9 m²
Total Floor Area   168.9 m²
Photographer   Hiroyuki Hirai
Further Reading   GG portfolio/Shigeru Ban

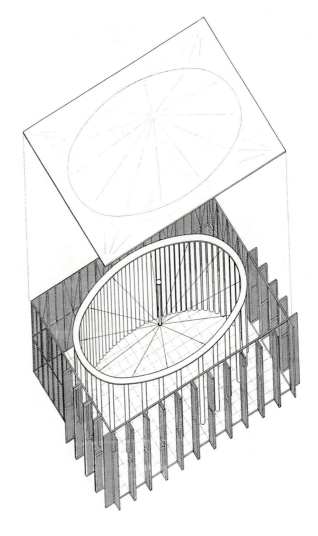

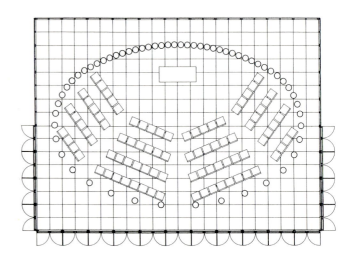

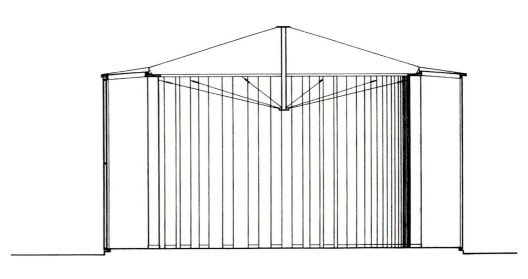

Akira Sakamoto, Osaka
Hakuei Residence

Osaka, Japan
June 1995–August 1996

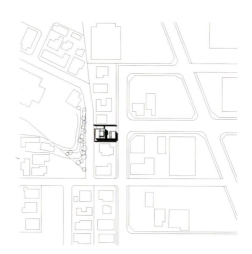

Award   JIA Prize for the Best Young Architect of the Year 1997
Given by   JIA The Japan Institute of Architects
Prize Presentation   September/22/1997
Members of the Jury   Koichi Nagashima, Waro Kishi, Norihiko Dan
Design Team   Akira Sakamoto
Structural Engineering   Arakawa Structural Design Office
Site Area   251.94 m²
Building Area   118.42 m²
Total Floor Area   178.55 m²
Photographer   Yoshiharu Matsumura

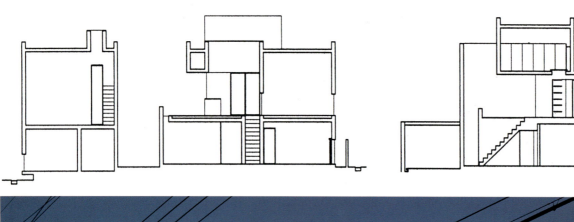

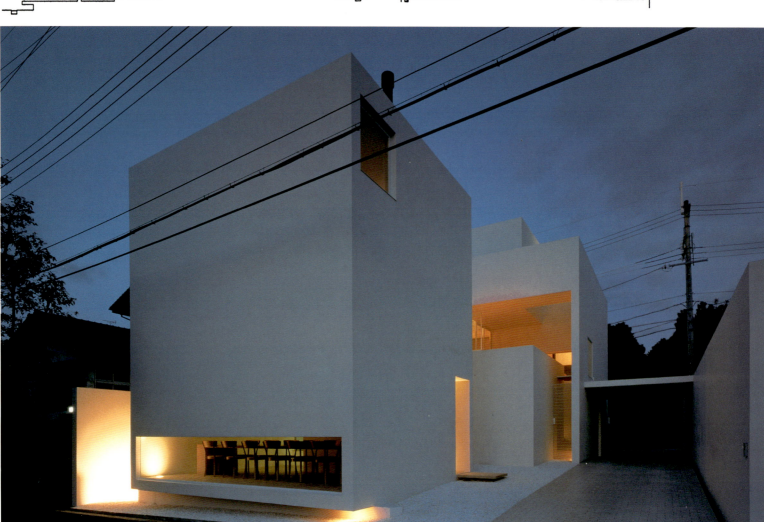

Kazuo Watabe, Tokyo
Kikyo Extended Care Facility
Affiliated to OTA General Hospital

Koriyama, Fukushima Prefecture, Japan
June 1994–May 1996

Award   JIA Prize for the Best Young Architect of the Year 1997
Given by   JIA The Japan Institute of Architects
Prize Presentation   September/22/1997
Members of the Jury   Koichi Nagashima, Waro Kishi, Norihiko Dan
Design Team   Yui Architects & Planners, Tokyo
Structural Engineering   Tohyama Architects & Engineers
Site Area   5,000 m²
Building Area   2,407 m²
Total Floor Area   3,987 m²
Photographer   Toshibumi Ogura

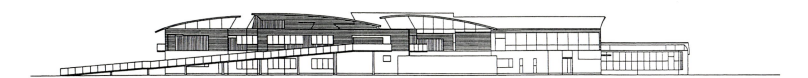

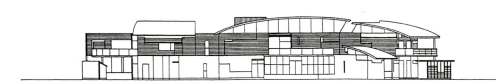

Du-Nam Choi, Seoul
Gallery SamTuh

ChoungDamDong, KangNamKu, Seoul, Korea
July 1994–August 1997

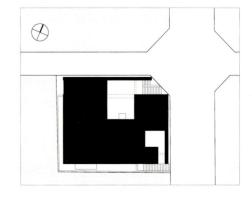

Award   20th Korean Institute of Architects Prize 1998
Given by   Korean Institute of Architects
Prize Presentation   February/16/1998
Members of the Jury   Jin Kyun Kim, Suk Woong Chang,
   Kil Ryong Park, Myung Won Chung, Young Gun Park
Design Team   DuNam Choi Architects + KunWon International Inc.
Structural Engineering   Kee Engineering
Mechanical Engineering   BoWoo Engineering
Electrical Engineering   MyongJin Engineering
Lighting Consultant   LiteWork
Interior Design   DuNam Choi Architects
Landscape Architecture   DuNam Choi Architects
Approximate Cost   WON/m² 1,200,000
Site Area   328.50 m²
Building Area   197.02 m²
Total Floor Area   1,151.97 m²
Photographer   YongKwan Kim, ChungEui Lim
Further Reading   Korean Architects, October 1997

Nak Jung Kim – Jung Won Architects, Consultants & Engineers Co., Ltd., Seoul
Cine Plus Complex

Sinsa-Dong, Seoul, Korea
August 1995–December 1997

Award   20th Korean Institute of Architects Prize 1998
Given by   Korean Institute of Architects
Prize Presentation   February/16/1998
Members of the Jury   Jin Kyun Kim, Suk Woong Chang,
   Kil Ryong Park, Myung Won Chung, Young Gun Park
Design Team   Jin In Kim, Hyun Joo Suh, Soo Il Lee
Structural Engineering   Dong Yang Consulting Engineers Co., Ltd.
Mechanical Engineering   Hyunwoo MEC Co.
Electrical Engineering   Sukwoo Engineering Co.
Acoustic Engineering   Kang Ryuk Engineers Co.
Air Conditioning Consultant   Hyunwoo MEC Co.
Lighting Consultant   Sukwoo Engineering Co.
Life Safety Consultant   Hyundai Housing & Industrial Development Co., Ltd.
Interior Design   Hyundai Wood Industry Co., Ltd.
Approximate Cost   US$ 15,000,000
Site Area   1,460 m²
Building Area   854 m²
Total Floor Area   9,032 m²
Photographer   Tae Oh Kim
Further Reading   SPACE Art Magazine

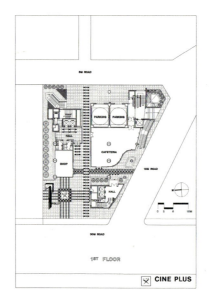

T. R. Hamzah & Yeang Sdn. Bhd., Selangor
Central Plaza
34 Jalan Sultan Ismail, Kuala Lumpur, Malaysia
1992–1996

Award   PAM Architecture Award 1997 (Commercial Category)
Given by   PAM Pertubuhan Akitek Malaysia
Prize Presentation   September/27/1997
Members of the Jury   President PAM & Chairman, Panels of Assessors
Design Team   Ken Yeang (Principal in Charge), Lim Piek Boon, Yew Ai Choo (Project Architects), Rachel Atthis, Azahari Muhammad (Design Architects), Rachel Atthis, Paul Brady, Tim Mellor Russell Harnnet (Design Development Architects)
Structural Engineering   Reka Peruding Sdn. Bhd.
Civil Engineering   Reka Perunding Sdn. Bhd.
Mechanical Engineering   Jurutera Perunding LC. Sdn. Bhd.
Electrical Engineering   Jurutera Perunding LC. Sdn. Bhd.
Air Conditioning Consultant   Mulpha Engineering & Construction Sdn. Bhd.
Lighting Consultant   Architectural Lighting Services Sdn. Bhd.
Interior Design   T. R. Hamzah & Yeang Designs Sdn. Bhd.
Quantity Surveying   Baharuddin All & Low Sdn
Approximate Cost   RM 49,000,000
Site Area   2,982.5 m²
Total Floor Area   57,863 m²
Photographer   KLNg Photography
Further Reading   Architectural Review, September 1996

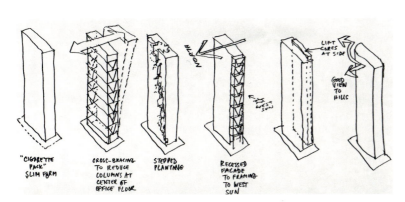

Claus en Kaan Architecten, Amsterdam
Binnen Wieringerstraat
Amsterdam, The Netherlands
1990–1995

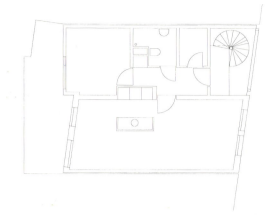

Award   Grand Prix Rhénan d'Architecture 1997
Given by   BNA Bond van Nederlandse Architekten, BDA Bund Deutscher
   Architekten Rheinland-Pfalz, Conseil National de l'Ordre des Architectes, BSA
Prize Presentation   July/10/1997
Members of the Jury   François Loyer (Chairman), André Bruder, Katharina
   Knapkiewics, Pierre Bonnet, Ad Turns, Meindert Booy, Jochem Jourdan,
   Gerhard Freising, Bruno Decaris, Bruno Fortier, Guy Hilbert
Design Team   Michiel van Pelt, Roland Rens, Floor Arons
Structural Engineering   Bouwadviesburo Strackee, Amsterdam
Approximate Cost   Fl. 1,450,000
Photographer   Ger van der Vlugt, Amsterdam
Further Reading   A + U April 1996
Commissioner   De Principaal

Oosterhuis Associates, Rotterdam
Garbage Transfer Station – Elhorst/Vloedbelt

Zenderen, The Netherlands
1993–1995

Award   Océ/BNA Prize for Industrial Architecture 1996
Given by   BNA Bond van Nederlandse Architekten
Prize Presentation   December/2/1996
Members of the Jury   C. Berendsen (Chairman), J.C. Blankert,
    L.A. Geelhoed, P.G. Vermeulen, A. Tuns
Design Team   Kas Oosterhuis (Project Architect), Ilona Lénárd,
    Leo Donkersloot, Menno Rubbens, Niek van Vliet, Jeroen Huijsinga
Supervision   Bouw Consulting Twente, Enschede
Management   Berenschot Osborne, Utrecht
Structural and Mechanical Engineering   Heijmans Industries
    Services Zuid, Rosmalen
Electrical Engineering   Rossmark, Almelo
Interior Design   Oosterhuis Associates
Approximate Cost   Fl. 7,850,000
Total Floor Area   5,490 m²
Building Area   5,490 m²
Photographer   Hans Werlemann (ground views),
    Photo Holland (aerial view)
Further Reading   De architect, December 1995,
    pp. 36–41, ISSN 0044–8621

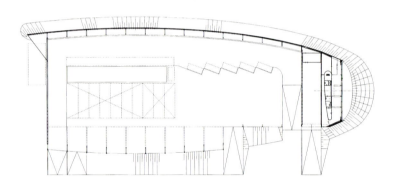

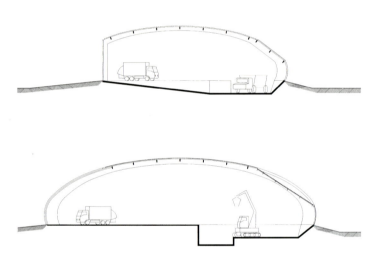

Sverre Fehn, Oslo
The Aukrust Centre
Alvdal, Norway
1992–1996

Award   Statens Byggeskikkpris 1997
Given by   Norske Arkitekters Landforbund
Prize Presentation   October/28/1997
Members of the Jury   Nina Kielland (Leader), Ole Hovland, Knut Hjeltness
Collaborator   Henrik Hille
Structural Engineering   Terje Orlien AS
Services Engineering   Oddvár Hegge AS
Electrical Engineering   Gunnar Eigil Støltun
Interior Design   Sverre Fehn, Henrik Hille, Erik Strandskogen
Landscape Architecture   Bjarne Aasen

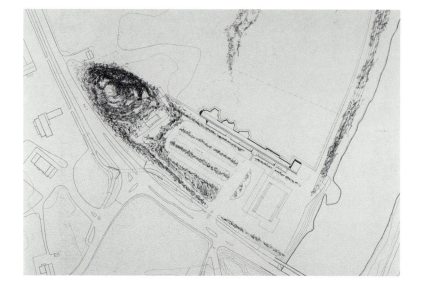

Gapp Architects and Urban Designers, Johannesburg
Park Hyatt Hotel
Johannesburg, South Africa
1993–1996

Award   SAIA Award of Merit 1997
Given by   SAIA South African Institute of Architects
Prize Presentation   November/17/1997
Members of the Jury   Hannah Le Roux, Italo Lupini, William Martinson,
   Jennifer Sorrell, Clive van den Berg
Design Team   Chris Kroese, Barry Senior, Glen Gallagher, Johan Smith,
   Karen Mailer, Carl Kruger
Structural Engineering   Arup Consulting Engineers
Mechanical Engineering   DLV Incorporated
Electrical Engineering   Repete Electrical Services (Pty.) Ltd.
Acoustic Engineering   H.E. Hanrahan
Air Conditioning Consultant   DLV Incorporated
Lighting Consultant   Paul Pamboukian & Associates
Interior Design   Hirsch Bedner Associates
Landscape Architecture   OVP Associates
Quantity Surveying   Winkfield Projects
Approximate Cost   R 100,000,000
Site Area   16,299 m^2
Building Area   8,734 m^2
Total Floor Area   30,309 m^2
Photographer   Costa Economides
Further Reading   South African Architect, Planning

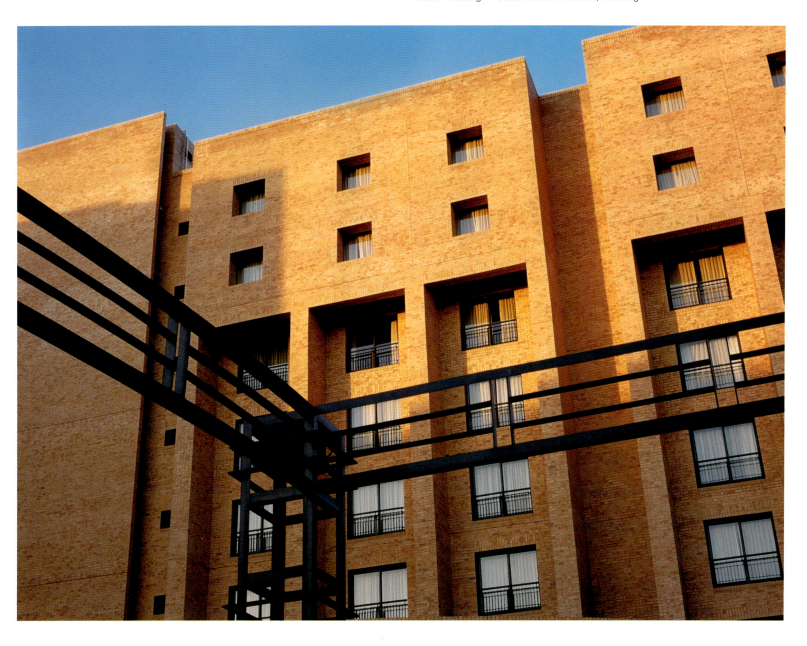

Louw Apostolellis Bergenthuin, Sandton
Siemens Park Phase 1
Midrand, South Africa
1994–1996

Award   SAIA Award of Merit 1997
Given by   SAIA South African Institute of Architects
Prize Presentation   November/17/1997
Members of the Jury   Hannah Le Roux, Italo Lupini, William Martinson,
   Jennifer Sorrell, Clive van den Berg
Structural Engineering   Van Niekerk, Kleyn & Edwards
Civil Engineering   Van Niekerk, Kleyn & Edwards
Mechanical Engineering   Spoormaker & Partners Inc.
Electrical Engineering   Claasen Auret Inc.
Contractor   Concor S.A.
Acoustic Engineering   Aluglass Hüppe
Air Conditioning Consultant   Aster
Lighting Consultant   Aster ECD
Life Safety Consultant   Midrand Fire Department/Bramley Morgado
Landscape Architecture   Patrick Watson & Grohovaz
Quantity Surveying   AUB Projects Pty. Ltd
Approximate Cost   R 70,000
Site Area   73,857 m²
Total Floor Area   23,450 m²
Photographer   Paolo De Liperi
Further Reading   SA Architect & Builder

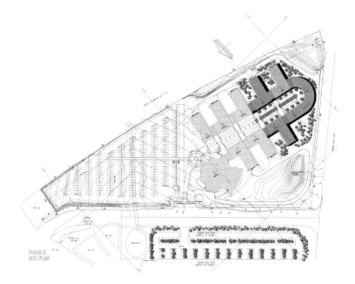

Meyer Pienaar, Bentel Abramson and Gapp, Johannesburg
Sandton Square

Sandton, South Africa
1993–1996

Award   SAIA Award of Merit 1997
Given by   SAIA South African Institute of Architects
Prize Presentation   November/17/1997
Members of the Jury   Hannah Le Roux, Italo Lupini, William Martinson,
   Jennifer Sorrell, Clive van den Berg
Design Team   François Pienaar, Alberto Reynoso, Hannes Niesen
Structural Engineering   Leech Price
Civil Engineering   Leech Price
Mechanical Engineering   Richard Pearce
Electrical Engineering   Claasen Auret
Environmental Engineering   Patrick Watson
Acoustic Engineering   Hugh Hanrahan
Air Conditioning Consultant   Richard Pearce
Lighting Consultant   Tony d'Olivera, Paul Pamboukian
Life Safety Consultant   WEVS
Interior Design   Lionel Levine (Hotel only)
Landscape Architecture   Patrick Watson
Quantity Surveying   Stocks Projects – John Cole
Approximate Cost   US$ 100,000,000
Site Area   23,406 m²
Building Area   140,000 m²
Total Floor Area   80,000 m²
Photographer   François H. Pienaar
Further Reading   Architecture SA, October 1996

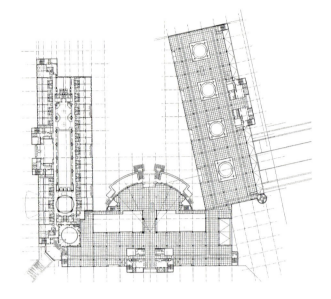

Alfio Torrisi Architects, Saxonwold
The Pharmaceutical Society of Southern Africa
Melrose, Johannesburg, South Africa
April 1996–February 1997

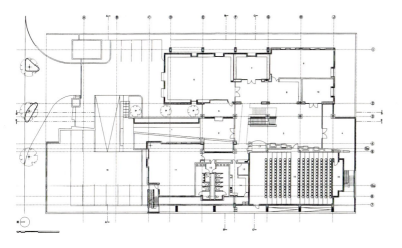

Award   SAIA Award of Merit 1997
Given by   SAIA South African Institute of Architects
Prize Presentation   November/17/1997
Members of the Jury   Hannah Le Roux, Italo Lupini, William Martinson,
  Jennifer Sorrell, Clive van den Berg
Design Team   Alfio Torrisi, Antony Abate, Christian Gottschalk
Structural Engineering   Huff Border Smith and Associates
Electrical Engineering   Rawlins Wales and Partners
Air Conditioning Consultant   Richard Pearce and Partners
Lighting Consultant   Streamlight
Landscape Architecture   Leaf Architects
Quantity Surveying   Cronge de Jager Partnership
Approximate Cost   R 7,600,000
Site Area   2,989 m²
Building Area   1,295 m²
Total Floor Area   4,010 m²
Photographer   Costa Economides
Further Reading   South African Architect

Foster and Partners, London
Bilbao Metro

Bilbao, Spain
1987–1995

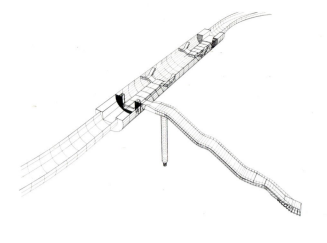

Award   III Premio Manuel de la Dehesa (Finalista)
Given by   Consejo Superior de los Colegios de Arquitectos de España
Prize Presentation   1996
Client   Basque Government – Department of Transportation and Public Works,
    Vitoria
Project Coordination, Engineering and Construction Management   IMEBISA, Bilbao
System Planning Infrastructure and Engineering   Sener, Bilbao; TYPSA, Madrid
PROJECT TEAM
Competition Team 1987–1988
Architects   Sir Norman Foster and Partners – Norman Foster, Spencer de Grey,
    David Nelson, Rodney Uren, Michael Borinski, Mark Bramhall
Lighting   Claude Engle Lighting, Washington D.C.
Signage   Otl Aicher, Rotis
Production Information Team 1988–1991
Architects   Sir Norman Foster and Partners – Norman Foster, David Nelson,
    Rodney Uren, Mary Bowman, Gerard Evenden, Nigel Greenhill, Ken Gómez,
    John MacFarland, Alex Trussov
Architects Consultants:
Concrete Consultant   Ove Arup & Partners, Arup Design and Research
Tunnel Engineering   Mott, Hay, Anderson, London
Lighting Consultant   Claude Engle Lighting, Washington D.C.
Signage   Otl Aicher, Rotis; Hans-Jorg Brücklacher
Quantitiy Surveyor   Davis Langdon & Everest, London
Construction Team 1991–1995
Architects   Sir Norman Foster and Partners – Norman Foster, David Nelson,
    Rodney Uren, Mary Bowman, Kevin Carrucan, Etienne Borgos, Nigel Greenhill
Civil Works Contractors   UTE Fomento-Balzola; Agromán; Dragados; Entrecanales;
    LAIN:Urruticoechea
Precast Panels   POSTENSA; Bilbao
Fit-out Contratcors:
Mezzanines   SENER (Engineering); Ferrovial (General Contractor); URSSA
    (Fabrication)
Entrance Canopies   SAITEC (Engineering); FOLCRA (Fabrication); URSSA
    (Fabrication)
Lightweight Metalwork   Ferrovial; URSSA
Paving Finishes   Sobrino
Signage and Furniture   Michael Weiss Associates (Design); Acaba (Fabrication)
Size   60 km length approx. comprising single underground line connecting
    to existing surface line
Approximate Cost   £ 577,000,000
Photographer   Richard Davies
Further Reading   Architectural Review, May 1997

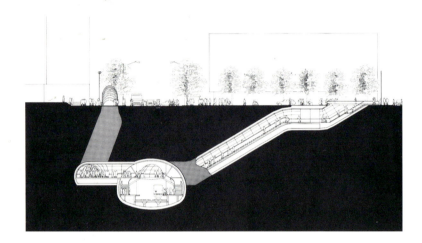

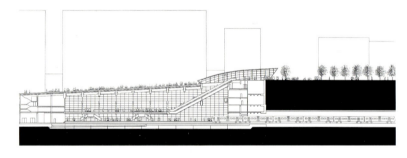

Maria Fraile, Javier Revillo, Madrid
Recinto Ferial

Zamora, Spain
1993–1996

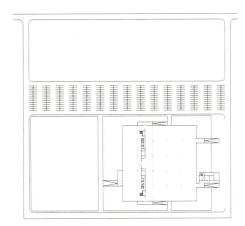

Award   IV Bienal de Arquitectura Española 1995–1996
Given by   Consejo Superior de los Colegios de Arquitectos de España;
   Ministerio de Fomento; Universidad Internacional Menéndez y Pelayo;
   Universidad de Alcalá
Prize Presentation   July/17/1997
Members of the Jury   Carlos Ferrater, Antonio Cruz, Gerardo Mingo Pinacho,
   Roberto Ercilla Abaitua, Isabel León, Jordi Garcés, Luis Fernández-Galiano,
   Juan Herreros, Joaquín Ibáñez
Design Team   Maria Fraile, Javier Revillo
Structural Engineering   Luis Lasic
Mechanical Engineering   J.G. & Asociados
Electrical Engineering   J.G. & Asociados
Air Conditioning Consultant   J.G. & Asociados
Lighting Consultant   J.G. & Asociados
Interior Design   Maria Fraile, Javier Revillo
Landscape Architecture   Maria Fraile, Javier Revillo
Approximate Cost   PTA 801,000,000
Site Area   60,000 m²
Building Area   8,000 m²
Total Floor Area   11,000 m²
Photographer   Luis Asin
Further Reading   El croquis, no. 81/82

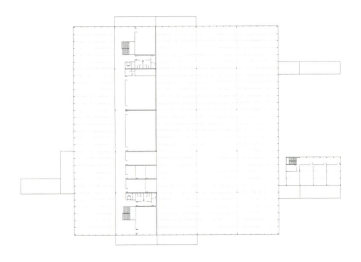

José Manuel Gallego Jorreto, La Coruña
Museum of Fine Art

La Coruña, Galicia, Spain
1988–1995

Award   IV Bienal de Arquitectura Española
Given by   Consejo Superior de los Colegios de Arquitectos de España; Ministerio de Fomento; Universidad Internacional Menéndez y Pelayo; Universidad de Alcalá
Prize Presentation   July/17/1997
Members of the Jury   Carlos Ferrater, Antonio Cruz, Gerardo Mingo Pinacho, Roberto Ercilla Abaitua, Isabel León, Jordi Garcés, Luis Fernández-Galiano, Juan Herreros, Joaquín Ibáñez
Design Team   Jose Manuel Gallego Jorreto, Eduardo Gonzalez Amores, Enrique Rodriguez, Carlos Quintans, Evaristo Zas, Juan Creus
Structural Engineering   J. Andujar (Project), J.M. Cidoncha
Mechanical Engineering   F. Luis Ara
Air Conditioning Consultant   Fluterga
Lighting Consultant   Montero
Life Safety Consultant   ERCO
Interior Design   Jose Manuel Gallego Jorreto
Landscape Architecture   Jose Manuel Gallego Jorreto
Approximate Cost   PTA 800,000,000
Site Area   2,500 m²
Building Area   5,776 m²
Photographer   Pablo Gallego
Further Reading   Museo de Belas Artes Da Coruña, M. Gallego, Ed. Xunta de Galicia, 1996

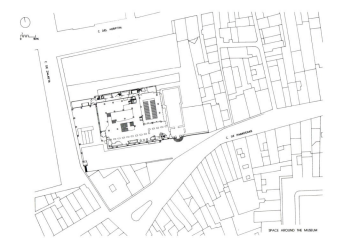

JJ-PP y Asociados, S.L. – Jerónimo Junquera, Estanislao Pérez Pita, Madrid
Office Building and Computing Centre for the Caja Madrid Savings Bank

Las Rozas, Madrid, Spain
April 1991–1995

Award   IV Bienal de Arquitectura Española
Given by   Consejo Superior de los Colegios de Arquitectos de España; Ministerio de Fomento; Universidad Internacional Menéndez y Pelayo; Universidad de Alcalá
Prize Presentation   July/17/1997
Members of the Jury   Carlos Ferrater, Antonio Cruz, Gerardo Mingo Pinacho, Roberto Ercilla Abaitua, Isabel León, Jordi Garcés, Luis Fernández-Galiano, Juan Herreros, Joaquín Ibáñez
Design and Interior Team   Project: Jeronimo Junquera, Estanislao Pérez Pita, Liliana Obal (Collaborator); Site Supervision: Jeronimo Junquera, Liliana Obal, Paloma Lasso de la Vega (Collaborator)
Structural Engineering   Luis Alfonso Gomez Gaite
Mechanical Engineering   Estein, S.A.
Electrical Engineering   Estein, S.A.
Environmental Engineering   Estein, S.A.
Acoustic Engineering   Ove Arup & Partners, Madrid
Air Conditioning Consultant   Estein, S.A.
Lighting Consultant   Estein, S.A.
Landscape Architecture   Estudio Junquera – Pérez Pita, Arquitectos
Quantity Surveying   Fernando Vasco Hidalgo, Lucinio Pérez Rodriguez, Antonio Rodriguez Romero, Jesus Moreno Conejo
Approximate Cost   PTA 3,770,000,000
Site Area   37,431 m²
Building Area   20,000 m² (Office Space), 10,000 m² (Computing Centre), 28,000 m² (Services, Parking & Equipment)
Total Floor Area   58,000 m²
Photographer   Javier Azurmendi, Eduardo Sanchez
Further Reading   Bauwelt no. 31/32, Stuttgart 1996

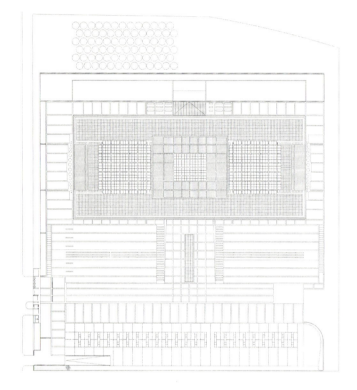

Josep Llinas Carmona, Barcelona
Instituto de Ensenanza Secundaria

Torredembarra, Spain
1993–1996

Award   IV Bienal de Arquitectura Española
Given by   Consejo Superior de los Colegios de Arquitectos de España;
  Ministerio de Fomento; Universidad Internacional Menéndez y Pelayo;
  Universidad de Alcalá
Prize Presentation   July/17/1997
Members of the Jury   Carlos Ferrater, Antonio Cruz, Gerardo Mingo Pinacho,
  Roberto Ercilla Abaitua, Isabel León, Jordi Garcés, Luis Fernández-Galiano,
  Juan Herreros, Joaquín Ibáñez
Design Team   Josep Llinas Carmona
Structural Engineering   Robert Brufau Niubo
Civil Engineering   Jaume Marti Almestoy
Mechanical Engineering   Lola Queralt Gimeno
Electrical Engineering   Lola Queralt Gimeno
Environmental Engineering   Lola Queralt Gimeno
Heating   Lola Queralt Gimeno
Lighting Consultant   Lola Queralt Gimeno
Landscape Architecture   Josep Llinas Carmona
Approximate Cost   PTA 505,400,000
Site Area   10,079.60 m^2
Building Area   5,255.30 m^2
Total Floor Area   5,255.30 m^2
Photographer   Lourbes Jansana Ferrer
Further Reading   Josep Llinàs, Editorial Tanaïs Ediciones,
  Sevilla 1997, pp. 140–151

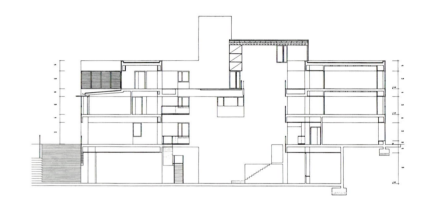

Sol Madridejos, Juan Carlos Sancho Osinaga, Madrid
Polideportivo Valvanera

San Sebastian de los Reyes, Madrid, Spain
1991–1996

Award   IV Bienal de Arquitectura Española
Given by   Consejo Superior de los Colegios de Arquitectos de España;
   Ministerio de Fomento; Universidad Internacional Menéndez y Pelayo;
   Universidad de Alcalá
Prize Presentation   July/17/1997
Members of the Jury   Carlos Ferrater, Antonio Cruz, Gerardo Mingo Pinacho,
   Roberto Ercilla Abaitua, Isabel León, Jordi Garcés, Luis Fernández-Galiano,
   Juan Herreros, Joaquín Ibáñez
Design Team   Sol Madridejos, Juan Carlos Sancho Osinaga
Structural Engineering   Juan Gutierrez
Approximate Cost   PTA 210,000,000
Site Area   3,250 m²
Building Area   2,350 m²
Total Floor Area   3,000 m²
Photographer   Hisao Suzuki, Eduardo Sanchez y Baltanás
Further Reading   El croquis, no. 81/82

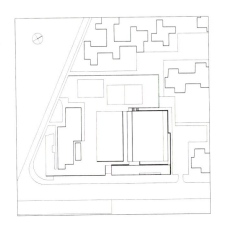 

Carmen Martinez Arroyo, Emilio Pemjean Muñoz, Rodrigo Pemjean Muñoz, Madrid
Town Hall, Clinic and Meeting Room

Madarcos, Madrid, Spain
1994–December 1996

Award   IV Bienal de Arquitectura Española
Given by   Consejo Superior de los Colegios de Arquitectos de España;
  Ministerio de Fomento; Universidad Internacional Menéndez y Pelayo;
  Universidad de Alcalá
Prize Presentation   July/17/1997
Members of the Jury   Carlos Ferrater, Antonio Cruz, Gerardo Mingo Pinacho,
  Roberto Ercilla Abaitua, Isabel León, Jordi Garcés, Luis Fernández-Galiano,
  Juan Herreros, Joaquín Ibáñez
Design Team   Carmen Martínez Arroyo, Emilio Pemjean Muñoz,
  Rodrigo Pemjean Muñoz
Site Management   Javier Mendez
Quantity Surveying   Maria Angeles Afonso
Approximate Cost   PTA 27,518,533
Building Area   308.16 m^2
Photographer   Angel Luis Baltanás, Eduardo Sanchez
Further Reading   AV Monografías 63–64, 1997

Joan Nogué, Txema Onzain, Jordi Roig, Barcelona
Nuns' Residence and Youth Hostel

Eguino, Alava, Spain
1994–1996

Award   IV Bienal de Arquitectura Española
Given by   Consejo Superior de los Colegios de Arquitectos de España; Ministerio
    de Fomento; Universidad Internacional Menéndez y Pelayo; Universidad de Alcalá
Prize Presentation   July/17/1997
Members of the Jury   Carlos Ferrater, Antonio Cruz, Gerardo Mingo Pinacho,
    Roberto Ercilla Abaitua, Isabel León, Jordi Garcés, Luis Fernández-Galiano,
    Juan Herreros, Joaquín Ibáñez
Design Team   Felix Lopez, Morten Lomholdt Architects
Structural Engineering   Robert Brufau i Associats
Civil Engineering   Robert Brufau i Associats
Lighting Consultant   ERCO
Interior Design   Joan Nogué, Txema Onzain, Jordi Roig
Landscape Architecture   Arantxa Iriarte
Quantity Surveying   Iñaqui Ondarra
Approximate Cost   PTA 200,000,000
Site Area   26,000 m²
Building Area   1,600 m²
Total Floor Area   3,050 m²
Photographer   C. Garcia, E. Armentia, F. López
Further Reading   Magasin A + T, no. 9, 1997, ISSN 1132–6409

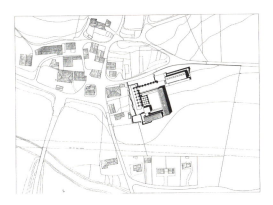

Álvaro Siza Vieira, Porto
Jardim de Santo Domingo de Bonaval
Santiago de Compostela, Spain
1989–1994

Award   III Prémio Manuel de la Dehesa 1997
Given by   IV Bienal de Arquitectura Española
Prize Presentation   July/17/1997
Design Team   Carles Muro, Alessandro D'Amico, Miguel Nery,
    João Sabugueiro, Joan Falgueras
Site Area   35,000 m²
Photographer   Roberto Cremascoli
Further Reading   Magazine Lotus, no. 88 (Italy)

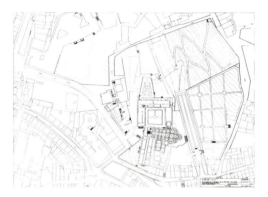

Álvaro Siza Vieira, Porto
Jardim de Santo Domingo de Bonaval
Santiago de Compostela, Spain
1989–1994

Tonet Sunyer i Vives, Barcelona
Sendín House
Madrid, Spain
1993–1995

Award   IV Bienal de Arquitectura Española
Given by   Consejo Superior de los Colegios de Arquitectos de España;
   Ministerio de Fomento; Universidad Internacional Menéndez y Pelayo;
   Universidad de Alcalá
Prize Presentation   July/17/1997
Members of the Jury   Carlos Ferrater, Antonio Cruz, Gerardo Mingo Pinacho,
   Roberto Ercilla Abaitua, Isabel León, Jordi Garcés, Luis Fernández-Galiano,
   Juan Herreros, Joaquín Ibáñez
Design Team   Tonet Sunyer, Luis Carreras, Eva Morral, Daniela Hartmann,
   Paco Varela, Eduard Doce
Structural Engineering   Eduard Doce
Civil Engineering   Paco Varela
Interior Design   Tonet Sunyer, Eva Morral, Daniela Hartmann
Quantity Surveying   Paco Varela
Approximate Cost   PTA 80,000,000
Site Area   3,000 m²
Building Area   750 m²
Total Floor Area   900 m²
Photographer   Luis Baltanas
Further Reading   El croquis, no. 76

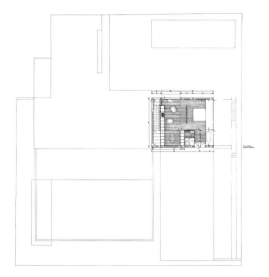

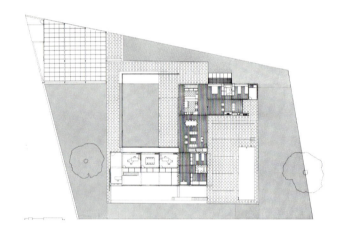

Guillermo Vázquez Consuegra, Seville
Instituto Andaluz del Patrimonio Histórico

Seville, Spain
1997

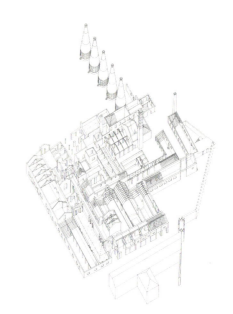

Award   IV Bienal de Arquitectura Española
Given by   Consejo Superior de los Colegios de Arquitectos de España;
   Ministerio de Fomento; Universidad Internacional Menéndez y Pelayo;
   Universidad de Alcalá
Prize Presentation   July/17/1997
Members of the Jury   Carlos Ferrater, Antonio Cruz, Gerardo Mingo Pinacho,
   Roberto Ercilla Abaitua, Isabel León, Jordi Garcés, Luis Fernández-Galiano,
   Juan Herreros, Joaquín Ibáñez
Design Team   Joaquin Amaya, Andres Lopez, Jorge Vazquez Consuegra
Structural Engineering   Juan Rueda
Civil Engineering   Marcos Vazquez Consuegra, Carlos Vazquez Tatay
Mechanical Engineering   Master, S.A.
Electrical Engineering   Master, S.A.
Environmental Engineering   Master, S.A.
Acoustic Engineering   Master, S.A.
Air Conditioning Consultant   Master, S.A.
Lighting Consultant   Master, S.A.
Life Safety Consultant   Marcos Vazquez Consuegra, Carlos Vazquez Tatay
Interior Design   Guillermo Vazquez Consuegra
Landscape Architecture   Guillermo Vazquez Consuegra
Quantity Surveying   Marcos Vazquez Consuegra
Approximate Cost   PTA 2,000,000,000
Site Area   10,000 m²
Building Area   5,700 m²
Total Floor Area   13,248 m²
Photographer   Duccio Malagamba
Further Reading   A + U Architecture and Urbanism,
   December 1996, no. 315

Ignacio Vicens y Hualde,
José Antonio Ramos Abengozar, Madrid
Edificio de Ciencias Sociales de la Universidad de Navarra

Pamplona, Spain
1994–1996

Award   1) IV Bienal de Arquitectura Española; 2) Premios COAVN de Arquitectura
Given by   1) Consejo Superior de los Colegios de Arquitectos de España, Ministerio de Fomento, Universidad Internacional de Menéndez Pelayo, Universidad de Alcalá; 2) Colegio Oficial de Arquitectos Vasco Navarro
Prize Presentation   1) July/17/1997; 2) 1997
Members of the Jury   1) Carlos Ferrater, Antonio Cruz, Gerado Mingo Pinacho, Roberto Ercilla Abaitua, Isabel León, Jordi Garcés, Luis Fernández-Galiano, Juan Herreros, Joaquín Ibáñez; 2) Rafael De Pedro Pérez-Salado, Jaime Allende Landa, José Mo Jimenéz Gurucharri, Javier Tellería Elorz, Luis Sesé Madrazo, José Manuel Pozo Municio, Fermín Alana Ortiz De Anda, Ignacio Gorostiaga Basterra, Miguel Arsuga Ballugera, Javier Martínez Oroquieta, Esteban Bonell
Design Team   Ignacio Vicens y Hualde, José Antonio Ramos Abengozar, Fernando Gil Castillo, Adam L. Bresnick
Structural Engineering   IDOM
Civil Engineering   IDOM
Mechanical Engineering   IDOM
Electrical Engineering   EIMAN
Environmental Engineering   IDOM
Acoustic Engineering   Noisetec
Air Conditioning Consultant   Norfrio

HLT, Henning Larsens Tegnestue A/S, Kopenhagen
Malmö Stadsbibliotek

Malmö, Sweden
1993–1998

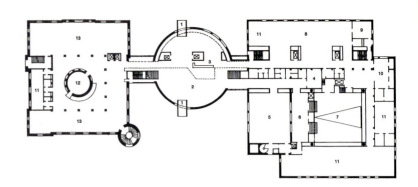

Award   Kasper Salin-Priset 1997
Given by   SAR Svenska Arkitekters Riksförbund
Prize Presentation   November/17/1997
Members of the Jury   Lars Asklund, Jan Berg, Gustaf Rosenberg, Stina Wallinder
Design Team   Henning Larsen, Niels Fuglsang (Project Manager), Louis Becker
   (Design Manager), Peer Teglgaard Jeppesen, Michael Christensen, Dorte Mandrup-
   Poulsen, Katrine Lotz, Hanne Halvorsen, Annika Carlsson, Hans Amos Christensen,
   Ingela Larsson, Jens Larsen, Mette Kynne Frandsen, Mette Carstad, Niels F. Turpie,
   Annette Jensen
Structural Engineering   J & W Bygg & Anläggning AB, Lidingö, Sweden
Civil Engineering   Travia AB, Malmö, Sweden
Mechanical Engineering   VVS-Gruppen AB, Lund, Sweden
Electrical Engineering   Sigma El- och Teleteknik, Malmö, Sweden
Acoustic Engineering   Jordan Akustik, Roskilde, Denmark
Interior Design   iA – Gruppen, Malmö, Sweden
Landscape Architecture   HLT in cooperation with Stig L. Andersson ApS
Approximate Cost   SEK 218,000,000
Site Area   10,000 m²
Building Area   3,300 m²
Total Floor Area   14,000 m² (gross)
Photographer   Jens Linde
Further Reading   1) MAMA no. 18, February 1998;
   2) Magasin för modern arkitektur, Stockholm

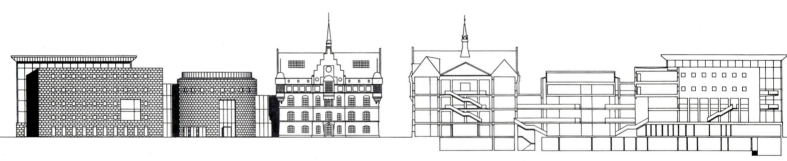

Alsop + Störmer Architects, London
Le Grand Bleu – Hôtel du Département
des Bouches-du-Rhône
Marseille, France

Award   RIBA Architecture Award (Europe)
Given by   RIBA The Royal Institute of British Architects
Prize Presentation   November/3/1997
Members of the Jury   Joanna van Heyningen, Rosalind Barwise, Marco
  Goldschmied, David Rock, Stephen Hodder
Design Team   Will Alsop, Stephen Fimbley, Francis Graves
Engineering   Arup International
Air Conditioning Consultant   Arup International
Lighting Consultant   Arup International
Life Safety Consultant   Jolyon Drury
Interior Design   Alsop; Rovræ-Bové; Andrée Putman
Landscape Architecture   Alsop + Störmer
Quantity Surveying   Hans Comb Ltd.
Approximate Cost   £ 115,000,000
Building Area   98,000 m²
Photographer   Paul Raftery (Arcaid)
Further Reading   Le Grand Bleu, Academy Editions

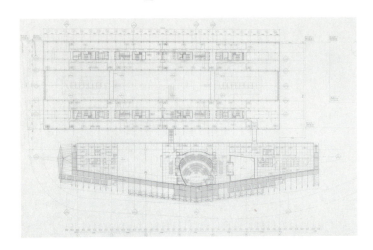

Armstrong Architects, London
La Maison de la culture du Japon à Paris
Paris, France
1992–1997

Award   RIBA Architecture Award (Europe)
Given by   RIBA The Royal Institute of British Architects
Prize Presentation   November/3/1997
Members of the Jury   Joanna van Heyningen, Rosalind Barwise,
    Marco Goldschmied, David Rock, Stephen Hodder
Structural Engineering   Groupe Arcora
Mechanical Engineering   Trouvin Ingenerie
Electrical Engineering   Trouvin Ingenerie
Acoustic Engineering   Xu Acoustique
Lighting Consultant   Isometrix
Theatre Consultant   Scene
Quantity Surveying   Algoe
Approximate Cost   FF 180,000,000 (excluding tax)
Site Area   1,670 m²
Building Area   9,000 m²
Total Floor Area   7,450 m²
Photographer   Philippe Ruault, Richard Davies, J. Armstrong
Further Reading   Kenchiku Bunka, Vol. 52, no. 611,
    September 1997

The Goddard Wybor Practice, Leeds
The Knavesmire Stand

York, United Kingdom
January 1994–May 1996

Award   RIBA Regional Architecture Award (Yorkshire)
Given by   RIBA The Royal Institute of British Architects
Prize Presentation   November/20/1997
Members of the Jury   Sir Philip Powell, Richard Dawson, Nigel Jenkins,
   Caryl Hubbard, Roman Piechocinski
Design Team   The Goddard Wybor Practice
Structural Engineering   White Young Green, Leeds
Mechanical Engineering   DSSR, Manchester
Electrical Engineering   DSSR, Manchester
Interior Design   The Goddard Wybor Practice
Landscape Architecture   The Goddard Wybor Practice
Quantity Surveying   Franklin & Andrews, Leeds
Approximate Cost   £ 11,350,000
Site Area   18,000 m²
Building Area   2,925 m²
Total Floor Area   10,270 m²
Photographer   DE Taylor, Martine Hamilton Knight

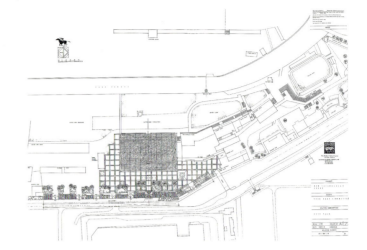

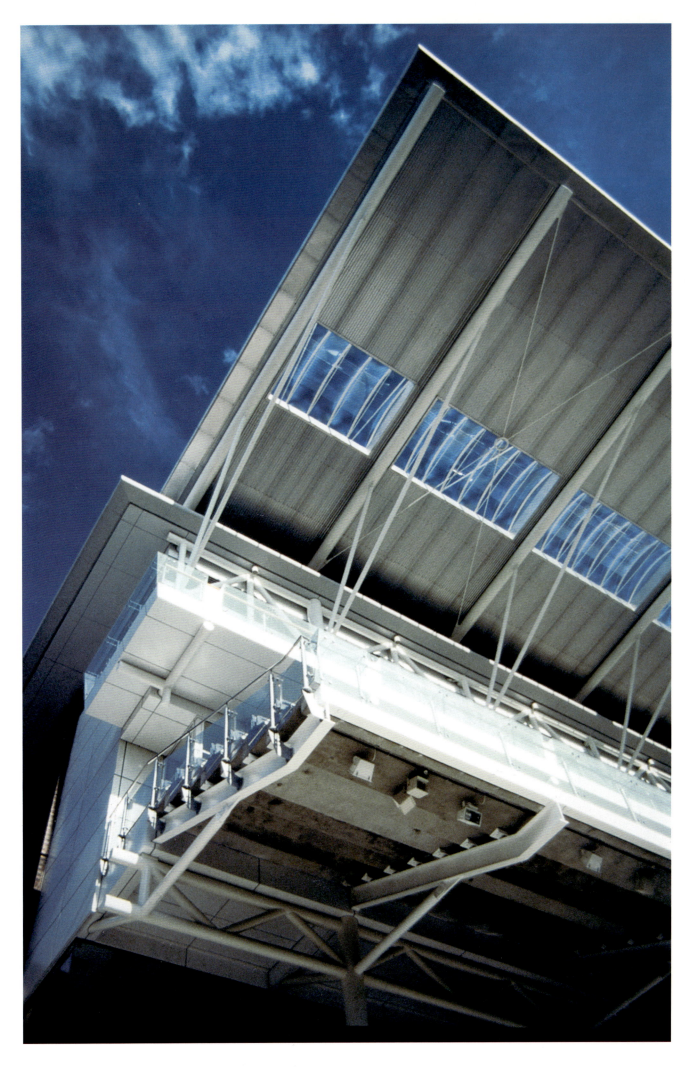

Nicholas Hare Architects, London
The Kempe Centre, Wye College, University of London
Wye, Kent, United Kingdom
September 1993–May 1996

Award   RIBA Regional Architecture Award (South East)
Given by   RIBA The Royal Institute of British Architects
Prize Presentation   October/15/1997
Members of the Jury   Jonathan Manser, Jeremy Reckless, Keith Barbour,
  Paul Beech, Richard Stilgoe
Design Team   Nicholas Hare, Sarah Jones, Darren Tims, Andrew Mulroy
Structural Engineering   Price & Myers
Mechanical Engineering   Atelier Ten
Electrical Engineering   Atelier Ten
Quantity Surveying   The Roger Wenn Partnership
Approximate Cost   £ 2,150,000
Site Area   4,690 m²
Building Area   1,400 m²
Total Floor Area   2,700 m²
Photographer   Dennis Gilbert
Further Reading   RIBA Journal, April 1997

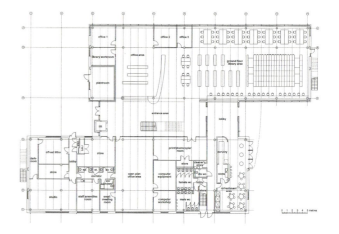

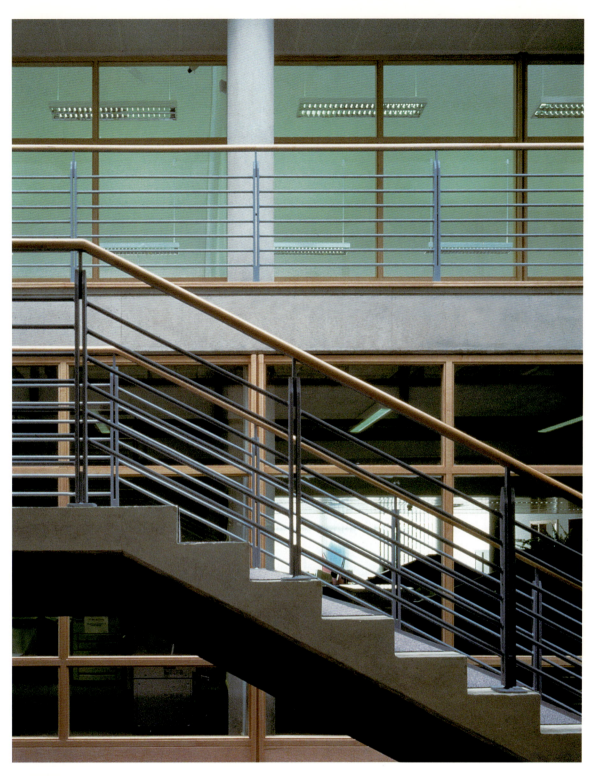

MacCormac Jamieson Prichard, London
Trinity College, Cambridge: Burrell's Field Development

Cambridge, United Kingdom
October 1989–September 1995

Award   RIBA Regional Architecture Award (Eastern)
Given by   RIBA The Royal Institute of British Architects
Prize Presentation   November 1997
Members of the Jury   David Morley (Chairman), Clive Jacobs (Lay Assessor),
   Frank Hawes (Regional Assessor)
Design Team   Richard MacCormac, Peter Jamieson, Michael Evans, David Bonta,
   Stephen Coomber, Gordon Fleming, Toby Johnson, Paul Mulligan, Oliver Smith,
   Edward Taylor, Reiner Langheit, Peter Hull
Structural Engineering   Harris & Sutherland, Cambridge
Civil Engineering   Harris & Sutherland, Cambridge
Mechanical Engineering   University of Cambridge, Estate Management
   and Building Service
Electrical Engineering   University of Cambridge, Estate Management
    and Building Service
Environmental Engineering   University of Cambridge,
   Estate Management and Building Service
Acoustic Engineering   Conrad Acoustics
Air Conditioning Consultant   University of Cambridge,
   Estate Management and Building Service
Lighting Consultant   University of Cambridge,
   Estate Management and Building Service
Interior Design   MacCormac Jamieson Prichard
Landscape Architecture   Cambridge Landscape Architects
Quantity Surveying   Davis Langdon and Everest, Cambridge
Site Area   20,500 m²
Building Area   2,429 m²
Total Floor Area   4,070 m²
Photographer   Peter Durant
Further Reading   The Architectural Review,
   Volume CCI, no. 1204, June 1997, pp. 66–71

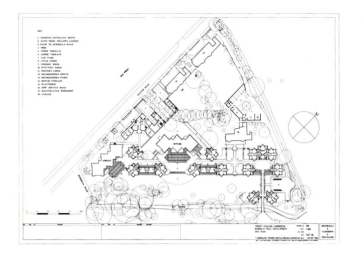

Shane O'Toole, Michael Kelly – Group 91 Architects, Dublin
The Ark – A Cultural Centre for Children
Temple Bar, Dublin, Ireland
1992–1995

Award   RIBA Architecture Award (Europe)
Given by   RIBA The Royal Institute of British Architects
Prize Presentation   November/3/1997
Members of the Jury   Joanna van Heyningen, Rosalind Barwise,
   Marco Goldschmied, David Rock, Stephen Hodder
Design Team   Shane O'Toole, Michael Kelly – Group 91 Architects, Susan Cogan
   (Assistant Architect), Santiago Calatrava (Design of Folding 'Theatre Curtain' Door)
Structural Engineering   KML Carl Bro
Mechanical Engineering   Homan O'Brien Associates
Electrical Engineering   Homan O'Brien Associates
Acoustic Engineering   Arup Acoustics
Historic Buildings Consultant   David Slattery
Theatre Consultant   Maurice Power
Fire Safety Consultant   John McCarthy
Artist   James Scanlon
Quantity Surveying   Seamus Monahan & Partners
Approximate Cost   IR£ 2,400,000
Site Area   350 m²
Building Area   300 m²
Total Floor Area   1,600 m²
Photographer   Keith Collie, Kevin Dunne, Shane O'Toole, John Searle
Further Reading   Temple Bar, The Power of an Idea, The Temple Bar
   Properties, Dublin 1996

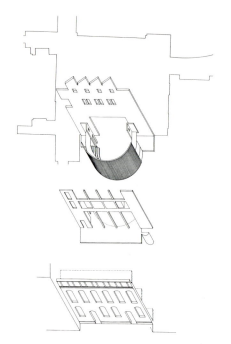

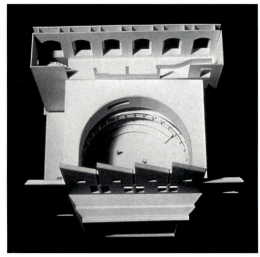

Sheppard Robson, London
The Helicon, 1 South Place

London, United Kingdom
September 1991–August 1996

Award   RIBA Regional Architecture Award (London)
Given by   RIBA The Royal Institute of British Architects
Prize Presentation   November/3/1997
Members of the Jury   Niall Philips, Elspeth Clements, Keith Price
Structural Engineering   John Savage Associates
Mechanical Engineering   Ove Arup & Partners
Electrical Engineering   Ove Arup & Partners
Environmental Engineering   Ove Arup & Partners
Acoustic Engineering   Arup Acoustics
Interior Design   Sheppard Robson
Landscape Architecture   Derek Lovejoy Partners
Quantity Surveying   Silk & Frazier
Approximate Cost   £ 30,000,000
Building Area   2,525 m² (max. footprint)
Total Floor Area   27,870 m² (gross external); 20,530 m² (net internal)
Photographer   Helicon: Richard Bryant, Peter Durant, Sheppard Robson
Further Reading   The Helicon, London 1996

Michael Wilford and Partners with James Stirling, London
Music School

Stuttgart, Germany
1986–1996

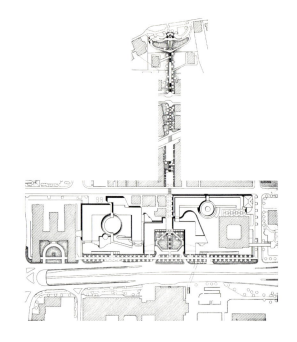

Award   RIBA Architecture Award (Europe), The Stirling Prize
Given by   RIBA The Royal Institute of British Architects
Prize Presentation   November/3/1997
Members of the Jury   Joanna van Heyningen, Rosalind Barwise, Marco Goldschmied, David Rock, Stephen Hodder
Design Team   Office personnel from both London and Stuttgart, including: Kenneth Beattie, Claire Bevington, John Bowmer, Brigit Class, Axel Deuschle, John Dorman, Felim Dunne, Klaus Fischer, Axel Funke, Irmgard Gassner, Stephan Gestner, Susan Haug, Wolfgang Heckman, Bernd Horn, Charlie Hussey, David Jennings, Daphne Kephalidis, Christian Kern, Michael Küpper, Steffen Lehman, Toby Lewis, Karin Ludewig, Marku Mangold, Philipp Misselwitz, Esmonde O'Brien, Rolf Ockert, Eilis O'Donnell, Peter Ray, John Rodgers, Ueli Schaad, Klaus-Jürgen Schnell, Manuel Schupp, Franziska Seeman, Philip Smithies, Rainer Strauss, Andrew Strickland, Karin Treutle, Richard Walker, Karen Waloschek, Frank Weisser, Siggi Wernik, Karenna Wilford, Denis Wolf, Eric Yim
Structural Engineering   Ove Arup and Partners, London; Boll and Partners, Stuttgart
Mechanical Engineering   Ove Arup and Partners, London; Jaeger Mornhinweg and Partners, Stuttgart
Electrical Engineering   Ove Arup and Partners, London; Ingenieurbüro S. Burrer, Stuttgart
Acoustic Engineering   Arup Acoustics, London; Müller BBM; Munich
Air Conditioning Consultant   Jaeger Mornhinweg and Partners, Stuttgart
Interior Design   Michael Wilford and Partners Limited
Approximate Cost   DM 90,000,000
Site Area   15,000 m²
Building Area   5,158 m²
Total Floor Area   20,830 m²
Photographer   Richard Bryant, ARCAID
Further Reading   Maxwell, Robert: Building: Formal inquiry: Stirling Wilford's Stuttgart Music School, In: Architecture Today, no. 72, London October 1996, pp. 20–30

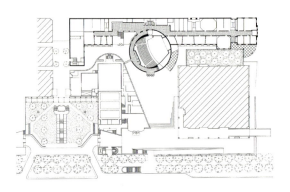

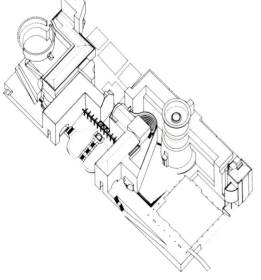

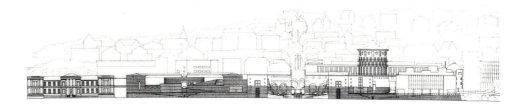

Chris Wilkinson Architects, London
Stratford Market Depot

Stratford, London, United Kingdom
May 1991–April 1996

Award   RIBA Commercial Architecture Award
Given by   RIBA The Royal Institute of British Architects
Prize Presentation   November/3/1997
Members of the Jury   Joanna van Heyningen, Rosalind Barwise,
   Marco Goldschmied, David Rock, Stephen Hodder
Design Team   Paul Baker, Zoe Barber, Dominic Bettison, Keith Brownlie,
   Stafford Critchlow, Simon Dodd (Project Architect Site), James Edwards
   (Project Architect Design Stages), Jim Eyre (Director in Charge), Stewart McGill,
   Nicola Smerin, Oliver Tyler, Chris Wilkinson, Jonathan Woodroffe
Structural Engineering   Hyder Consulting Ltd.
Civil Engineering   Hyder Consulting Ltd.
Mechanical Engineering   Hurley Palmer Partnership (formerly J.F. Hurley & Partners)
Electrical Engineering   Hurley Palmer
Environmental Engineering   Loren Butt
Landscape Architecture   Hyder Consulting Ltd., Chris Wilkinson Architects
Quantity Surveying   Hyder Consulting Ltd.
Approximate Cost   £ 25,000,000
Site Area   110,000 m²
Building Area   19,000 m²
Total Floor Area   22,000 m²
Photographer   Dennis Gilbert/View
Further Reading   Architectural Journal, July/31/1997 – August/7/1997

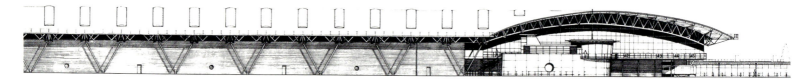

Derek Wylie Architecture, London
Lee House
London, United Kingdom

Award   RIBA Regional Architecture Award (London)
Given by   RIBA The Royal Institute of British Architects
Prize Presentation   November/3/1997
Members of the Jury   Niall Philips, Elspeth Clements, Keith Price
Design Team   Derek Wylie, Mike Neale, Carl Haper
Structural Engineering   Elliott Wood, London
Mechanical Engineering   Allen Hale Partnership Ltd.
Electrical Engineering   Allen Hale Partnership Ltd.
Environmental Engineering   Derek Wylie Architecture
Lighting Consultant   Derek Wylie Architecture
Life Safety Consultant   Derek Wylie Architecture
Interior Design   Derek Wylie Architecture
Landscape Architecture   Derek Wylie Architecture
Quantity Surveying   Martin Lee Associates
Approximate Cost   £ 300,000
Site Area   145 m²
Building Area   130 m²
Total Floor Area   250 m²
Photographer   Nick Kane Architectural Photography
Further Reading   Pierre, Catherine: Patio à Londres,
   Le Moniteur Architecture AMC, Paris, June 1997, no. 223

Renzo Piano Building Workshop, Genova
Jean-Marie Tjibaou Cultural Centre
Noumea, New Caledonia
1991–1998

Award   1998 Pritzker Architecture Prize
Given by   The Hyatt Foundation
Prize Presentation   June/16/1998
Members of the Jury   J. Carter Brown (Chairman), Giovanni Agnelli, Charles Correa,
   Ada Louise Huxtable, Toshio Nakamura, Jorge Silvetti, The Lord Rothschild (Juror
   Emeritus), Bill Lacy (Executive Director)
Design Team   P. Vincent (associate in charge), D. Rat, W. Vassal, M. Henry,
   J.B. Mothes, G. Modolo, A. El Jerari, A. Gallissian, AH. Téménidès, F. Pagliani,
   O. Doizy, A. Chaaya, D. Mirallie
Structural Engineering and Ventilation   Ove Arup & Partners (A. Guthrie, M. Banfi)
Ethnological Consultant   A. Bensa
Acoustic Engineering   Peutz
Cost Control   GEC (F. Petit, C. Baché)
Approximate Cost   FF 200,000,000
Site Area   80,000 m²
Total Floor Area   7,650 m²
Photographer   John Gollings, William Vassal
Further Reading   Renzo Piano Logbook, London 1997

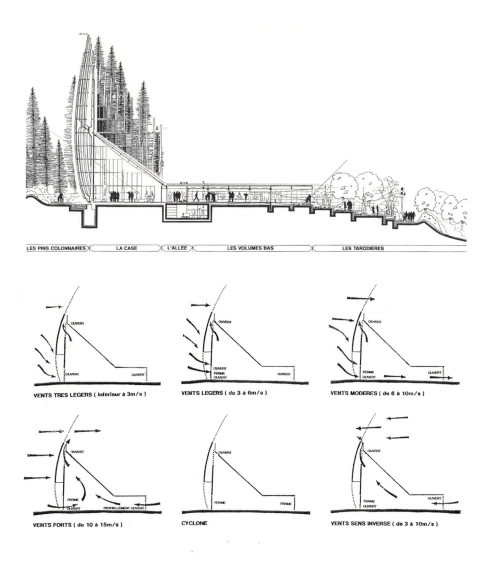

LES PINS COLONNAIRES | LA CASE | L'ALLEE | LES VOLUMES BAS | LES TARODIERES

VENTS TRES LEGERS (inférieur à 3m/s)

VENTS LEGERS (de 3 à 6m/s)

VENTS MODERES (de 6 à 10m/s)

VENTS FORTS (de 10 à 15m/s)

CYCLONE

VENTS SENS INVERSE (de 3 à 10m/s)

Manville Hall Student Apartments

Berkeley, California, USA
1992–1995

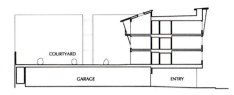

NORTH / SOUTH BUILDING SECTION

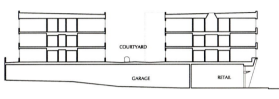

EAST / WEST BUILDING SECTION

Award   AIA National Honor Award for Architecture 1997
Given by   AIA The American Institute of Architects
Prize Presentation   May/18/1997
Members of the Jury   Malcolm Holzman (Chair), F. Michael Ayles, Dana Cuff, Joan E. Goody, Aaron E. Johnson, Susan Henshaw Jones, Robert L. Thompson, Anne G. Tyng, Robert Yudell
Design Team   David Baker, DeWitt Brock, Jane Snyder-Sac, Christine Kiesling
Structural Engineering   Steven Tipping & Associates
Civil Engineering   Kerry Engineering
Mechanical Engineering   JYA Consulting Engineers
Electrical Engineering   HCP Electrical Consulting
Geotechnical Engineering   Geomatrix Consultants
Landscape Architecture   Delaney & Cochran
Approximate Cost   US$ 7,300,000
Site Area   2,023 m²
Total Floor Area   6,600.75 m²
Photographer   Tom Rider
Further Reading   Architectural Record, May 1997, p. 76

Brayton & Hughes, Design Studio, San Francisco
Boyd Lighting Headquarters
San Francisco, California, USA

Award   AIA National Honor Award for Architecture 1997
Given by   AIA The American Institute of Architects
Prize Presentation   May/18/1997
Members of the Jury   Malcolm Holzman (Chair), F. Michael Ayles,
    Dana Cuff, Joan E. Goody, Aaron E. Johnson, Susan Henshaw Jones,
    Robert L. Thompson, Anne G. Tyng, Robert Yudell
Design Team   Richard Brayton, David Darling, Ross Dugan
Structural Engineering   Steve Tipping & Associates
Mechanical Engineering   Steve Tipping & Associates
Electrical Engineering   Dodt Electric
Showroom Consultant   Vanderbyl Design
Lighting Consultant   Chris Ripman Lighting
Interior Design   Brayton & Hughes, Design Studio
Metal Fabrication   Patrick Fitzgerald
Total Floor Area   1,021.8 m²
Photographer   John Sutton
Further Reading   Architectural Record, May 1997

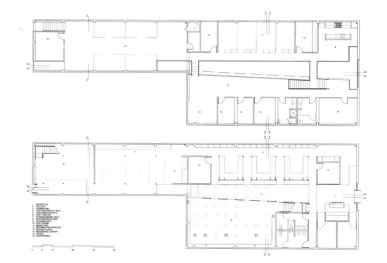

François de Menil Architect, P.C., New York; Bergmeyer Associates, Inc., Boston
Bottega Veneta, The Copley Place Mall

Boston, Massachusetts, USA
May 1995–November 1995

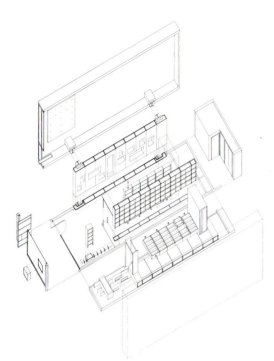

Award   AIA National Honor Award for Interiors 1997
Given by   AIA The American Institute of Architects
Prize Presentation   May 1997
Members of the Jury   Margaret McCurry, James R. Biber, Morrison Cousins, Susan Grant Lewin, Toshiko Mori
Design Team   François de Menil (Principal in Charge), James Moustafellos (Project Architect), Vicken Arslanian, John Blackmon, Jan Greben, Stephen Leventis, Stephen Mullins, Lavinia Pana (Project Team); Bergmeyer Associates, Inc. – Nina Monastero (Senior Associate)
Engineering Consultant   Z de Company (Mohammed Zade, Muzzafer Muctehitzade, Mezlut Koymen)
Lighting Consultant   Fisher Marantz Renfro Stone – Paul Marantz (Principal), Barry Citrin, E. Sara McBarnette
Glass Consultant   James Carpenter Design Associates – James Carpenter (Principal)
Glass Box Fabrication   Keer Design (Michael Scheiner)
Total Floor Area   84 m²
Photographer   Paul Warchol Photography, New York
Further Reading   Architectural Record, May 1996

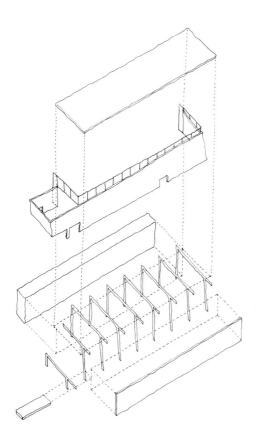

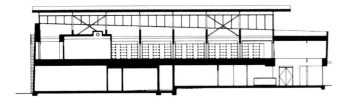

Steven Ehrlich Architects, Santa Monica
Paul Cummins Library, Crossroads School
Santa Monica, California, USA
1995–1996

Award   AIA National Honor Award for Architecture 1997
Given by   AIA The American Institute of Architects
Prize Presentation   May/18/1997
Members of the Jury   Malcolm Holzman (Chair), F. Michael Ayles, Dana Cuff,
   Joan E. Goody, Aaron E. Johnson, Susan Henshaw Jones, Robert L. Thompson,
   Anne G. Tyng, Robert Yudell
Design Team   Steven Ehrlich, Nick Seierup, Brent Eckerman,
   Gantcho Batchkaron, Iris Regn
Structural Engineering   G.O. Dyer
Plumbing   Suttles Plumbing, Mechanical Corp.
Mechanical Engineering   Pacific Mechanical Contractors Inc.
Electrical Engineering   Zeller Electric Corp.
Lighting Consultant   Edward Efferon Lighting
Site Area   1,900 m²
Building Area   700 m²
Total Floor Area   1,200 m²
Photographer   Erhard Pfeiffer
Further Reading   L'arca, May 1997

Steven Ehrlich Architects, Santa Monica
Schulman Residence
Brentwood, California, USA
1989–1992

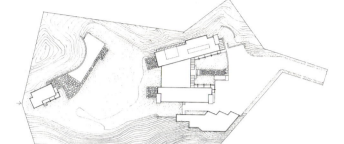

Award　AIA National Honor Award for Architecture 1997
Given by　AIA The American Institute of Architects
Prize Presentation　May/18/1997
Members of the Jury　Malcolm Holzman (Chair), F. Michael Ayles, Dana Cuff, Joan E. Goody, Aaron E. Johnson, Susan Henshaw Jones, Robert L. Thompson, Anne G. Tyng, Robert Yudell
Design Team　Steven Ehrlich, Jim Schmidt, Mel Bernstein, Carlos Kitzinger
Structural Engineering　Steven Perlof Consulting Engineers
Civil Engineering　Engineering Technology
Mechanical Engineering　Jack Khalifeh
Electrical Engineering　Kim Electric
Air Conditioning Consultant　Malibu Heating
Interior Design　Luis Ortega Design Studio
Landscape Architecture　Robert Cornell Associates
Site Area　8,000 m²
Total Floor Area　900 m²
Photographer　Tom Bonner
Further Reading　Monograph

**Hugh Hardy – Hardy Holzman Pfeiffer Associates,
New York**
New Victory Theater

New York, N.Y., USA
opened 1995

Award   AIA Honor Award for Interiors 1997
Given by   AIA The American Institute of Architects
Prize Presentation   May 1997
Members of the Jury   Margaret McCurry, James R. Biber,
  Morrison Cousins, Susan Grant Lewin, Toshiko Mori
Approximate Cost   US$ 11,900,000
Building Area   3,320 m²
Photographer   Elliott Kaufman

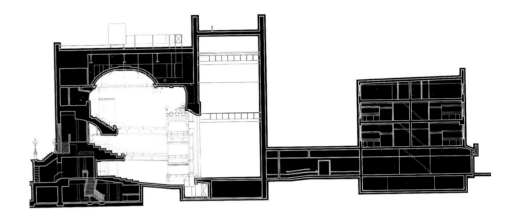

Herbert Lewis Kruse Blunck Architecture, Des Moines
Praxair Distribution, Inc.

Ankeny, Iowa, USA
January 1996–February 1997

Award   AIA National Honor Award for Architecture 1997
Given by   AIA The American Institute of Architects
Prize Presentation   May/18/1997
Members of the Jury   Malcolm Holzman (Chair), F. Michael Ayles, Dana Cuff,
    Joan E. Goody, Aaron E. Johnson, Susan Henshaw Jones, Robert L. Thompson,
    Anne G. Tyng, Robert Yudell
Design Team   Calvin F. Lewis, Stephen Knowles
Structural Engineering   Charles Saul Engineering, Des Moines
Mechanical Engineering   Stroh Corporation, Des Moines
Electrical Engineering   Stroh Corporation, Des Moines
Interior Design   Herbert Lewis Kruse Architecture
Approximate Cost   US$ 1,000,000
Building Area   5,684.8 m²
Total Floor Area   2,099 m² (office, conference and training);
    3,585.5 m² (warehouse and distribution)
Photographer   Farshid Assassi, Assassi Productions, Santa Barbara, California
Further Reading   Architecture Magazine, May 1997; Architectural Record,
    May 1997

Vincent James Associates Inc., Minneapolis
(Project initiated by James/Snow Architects Inc.)
Type/Variant House

Northern Wisconsin, USA
1994–1997

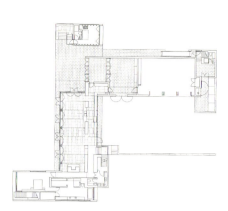

Award   AIA National Honor Award for Architecture 1998
Given by   AIA The American Institute of Architects
Prize Presentation   May/16/1998
Members of the Jury   Mark Simon, Walter F. Chatham, Susan F. Child, Bruce A.
  Eckfeldt, Michael Quinn, Adele Naude-Santos, Peter L. Schaudt, Scott A. Welch,
  Allison Williams, Robert Ziegelman
Design Team   Vincent James (Principal), Paul Yaggie (Project Architect),
  Nancy Blankfard, Nathan Knutson (Collaborators), Andrew Dull, Steve Lazen,
  Krista Scheib, Julie Snow, Taavo Somer, Kate Wyberg (Project Team)
Structural Engineering   McSherry Structural
Landscape Architecture   Coen + Stumpf
Site Area   22,779 m²
Building Area   714 m²
Total Floor Area   836 m²
Photographer   Don F. Wong, Mary Ludington
Further Reading   Northwoods Escape, In: Architecture Magazine,
  February 1997

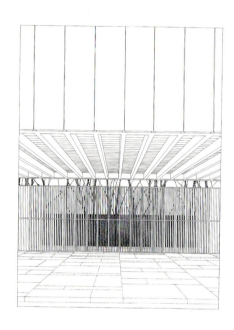

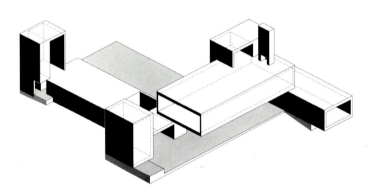

KressCox Associates P.C., Washington, DC
Connelly Chapel of Holy Wisdom of the Washington Theological Union

Washington, DC, USA
1994–1996

Award   AIA Religious Art and Architecture Design Award 1997
Given by   AIA The American Institute of Architects
Prize Presentation   September/20/1997
Members of the Jury   Walter F. Chatham, Errol Barron, Phillip T. Markwood,
   Kenneth von Roenn Jr., Bishop W.B. Spillman
Design Team   David Cox, Christoffer A. Graae, Steven Dickens, William Spack
Structural Engineering   Tadjer-Cohen-Edelson Associates, Inc.
Civil Engineering   VIKA
Mechanical Engineering   Schwartz Engineering
Electrical Engineering   Schwartz Engineering
Acoustic Engineering   Schwartz Engineering
Air Conditioning Consultant   Schwartz Engineering
Lighting Consultant   Light-n-Up
Life Safety Consultant   Schwartz Engineering
Interior Design   KressCox Associates
Landscape Architecture   VIKA
Quantity Surveying   Whiting Turner
Approximate Cost   US$ 750,000 (chapel only)
Site Area   6,517 m² (whole site)
Building Area   280 m² (chapel only)
Total Floor Area   236 m² (chapel only)
Photographer   Kenneth Wyner Photography
Further Reading   Environment and Art December 1996;
   The Washington Post, May/24/1997

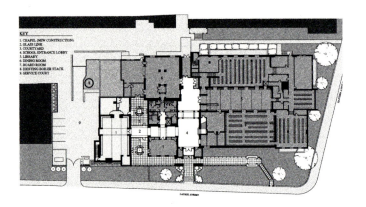

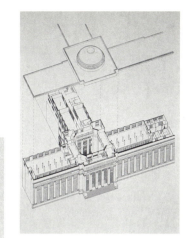

Leers Weinzapfel Associates, Boston
Massachusetts Institute of Technology School of Architecture and Planning
Cambridge, Massachusetts, USA
1994–1988

Award   AIA National Honor Award for Interiors 1998
Given by   AIA The American Institute of Architects
Prize Presentation   May/16/1998
Members of the Jury   Steven Goldberg, Heather Willson Cass, Hendrik Koning, Eva Maddox, Merry Norris
Design Team   Jane Weinzapfel (Principal in Charge), Andreas P. Leers (Consulting Principal), Akex Adkins, Mark Armstrong, Karen Moore, Karen Swett (Design Team), Lauren Dunn Rockhart, Catherine Lassen, Mee Lee (Project Team)
Structural Engineering   Lim Consultants, Inc.
Mechanical Engineering   TMP Consulting Engineers
Electrical Engineering   Lottero and Mason, Inc. (now part of TMP Consulting Engineers)
Acoustic Engineering   Cavanaugh and Tocci
Interior Design   LWA; Dthmer + Krabbendam (Consultant for Phase II)
Quantity Surveying   Kennedy and Rossi
Approximate Cost   US$ 7,000,000
Total Floor Area   4,243 m²
Photographer   Chick Choi
Further Reading   Artful Chesion, Architecture, August 1996

Edward I. Mills and Associates + Perkins Eastman and Partners, New York
Temple Beth Shalom Synagogue

Hastings-on-Hudson, New York, USA
completed 1995

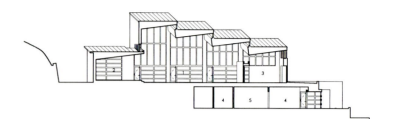

Award   AIA Religious Art and Architecture Design Award 1997
Given by   AIA The American Institute of Architects
Prize Presentation   September/20/1997
Members of the Jury   Walter F. Chatham, Errol Barron,
    Phillip T. Markwood, Kenneth von Roenn Jr., Bishop W.B. Spillman
Design Team   Edward I. Mills, Aaron B. Schwarz, Mauricio Salazar,
    Bradford Perkins
Structural Engineering   Feld, Kaminetzky and Cohen
Mechanical Engineering   Abe Joselow
Electrical Engineering   Abe Joselow
Environmental Engineering   Abe Joselow
Air Conditioning Consultant   Abe Joselow
Lighting Consultant   Edward I. Mills and Associates, Perkins Eastman and Partners
Interior Design   Edward I. Mills and Associates, Perkins Eastman and Partners
Landscape Architecture   David Ferris Miller
Approximate Cost   US$ 2,000,000
Site Area   14,260 m²
Building Area   1,500 m²
Total Floor Area   750 m²
Photographer   Chuck Choi Architectural Photography
Further Reading   Temple Beth Shalom,
    Faith and Form, Volume 30, no. 1, 1997

**PMG Architects – Peter M. Gumpel, New York;
in Association with STARCK – Philippe Starck,
Issy Les Moulineaux, France
Delano Hotel**

Miami Beach, Florida, USA

Award   AIA National Honor Award for Architecture 1997
Given by   AIA The American Institute of Architects
Prize Presentation   1997

Roth and Moore Architects, New Haven
Joseph Slifka Center for Jewish Life at Yale
New Haven, Connecticut, USA
1964–1995

Award   AIA Religious Art and Architecture Design Award 1997
Given by   AIA The American Institute of Architects
Prize Presentation   September/20/1997
Members of the Jury   Walter F. Chatham, Errol Barron, Phillip T. Markwood,
  Kenneth von Roenn Jr., Bishop W.B. Spillman
Design Team   Harold Roth, William F. Moore, Randall Luther, David Thompson,
  Laurence Odfjell, George Clemens, Amy Beierle, David Roth
Structural Engineering   Spiegel Zamenik & Shah, New Haven
Mechanical and Electrical Engineering   BVH Engineers, Bloomfield
Acoustic Engineering   Cavanaugh Tocci Associates, Sudbury
Landscape Architecture   Jack Curtis & Associates, Monroe
Cost Estimating   Ray Firmin, North Tarrytown
Approximate Cost   US$ 4,000,000
Site Area   772 m²
Building Area   513 m²
Total Floor Area   1,860 m²
Photographer   Jeff Goldberg – Esto Photographics

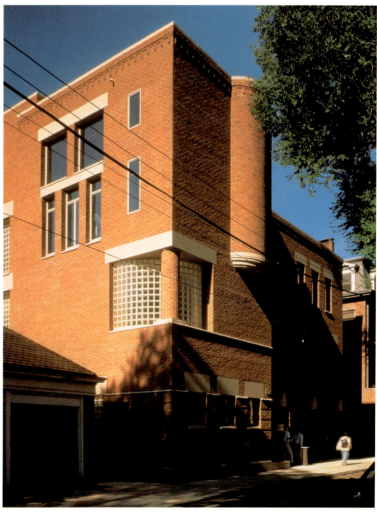

Salmela Architect – David D. Salmela, Duluth
Brandenburg's Ravenwood Studio

Ely, Minnesota, USA
1995–1997

Award AIA National Honor Award for Architecture 1998
Given by AIA The American Institute of Architects
Prize Presentation May/16/1998
Members of the Jury Mark Simon, Walter F. Chatham, Susan F. Child, Bruce A.
  Eckfeldt, Michael Quinn, Adele Naude-Santos, Peter L. Schaudt, Scott A. Welch,
  Allison Williams, Robert Ziegelman
Design Team David D. Salmela, Brad Holmes, Curt Holmes, Cheryl Fosdick
Structural Engineering Carroll & Franck; Hurst & Heinrichs
Interior Design Salmela Architects
General Construction Rod & Sons Carpentry
Landscape Architecture Coen & Stumpf & Associates
Kitchen and Bath Consultant Monson Interior Design
Site Area 500,000 m²
Building Area 285 m²
Total Floor Area 427 m²
Photographer Peter Kerze, Jim Brandenburg
Further Reading Architecture Magazine, May 1997;
  Architectural Record, May 1998

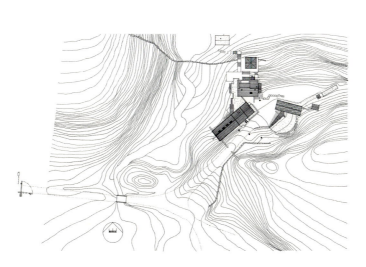

Skidmore, Owings & Merrill LLP, San Francisco
United States Court of Appeals

San Francisco, California, USA
1990–1995

Award   1) AIA National Honor Award for Architecture 1998; 2) AIA National Honor
Awards for Interiors 1998

Given by   AIA The American Institute of Architects

Prize Presentation   May/16/1998

Members of the Jury   Mark Simon, Walter F. Chatham, Susan F. Child, Bruce A.
Eckfeldt, Michael Quinn, Adele Naude-Santos, Peter L. Schaudt, Scott A. Welch,
Allison Williams, Robert Ziegelman

Design Team   Craig Hartman (Design Partner), Carolina Woo (Managing Partner),
Steve Weindel, Sharon Cox, Tom McMillan, Leo Chow, Jim Degener, Amy Coburn,
Mike McCone, Henry Vlanin, Philip Snyder, Nora Klebow, Dimitri Avdienko, Saturo
Kato, Bill White, Tob Herscoe, Richard Depp, Scott Dinsmore, John Hannah, Jessica
Rothschild, David Diamond, Ken Vais, Dave Larson, Hector Rubio, Elaine Stone

Project Manager   Ed McCrary, Fred Powell

Structural Engineering   Skidmore, Owings & Merrill LLP Navin Amin, Anoop Mokha,
Hamid Fatehi, Xiaosuan Qi, Ray Pugliesi, Dan Recurrel, Peter Lee, Emilio Alejandria,
Ernest Vayl

Mechanical Engineering   Flack & Kurtz, San Francicso

Electrical Engineering   Flack & Kurtz, San Francisco

Acoustic Engineering   Wilson, Ihrig & Associates Inc., Oakland

Lighting Consultant   Architectural Lighting Design, San Francisco

Interior Design   Skidmore, Owings & Merrill LLP Tamara Dinsmore, Chanda Capelli,
Bobbie Fisch, Wendy Chu

Graphic Design   Lonny Israel, Skidmore, Owings & Merrill LLP

Landscape Architecture   Patricia O'Brian Landscape Architects, San Francisco

Quantity Surveying   Hanscomb Associates. Inv. (Cost & Schedule), San Francisco

Base Isolation Consultant   Earthquake Protection Systems, Inc., Emeryville

Historic Architecture Consultant   Page & Turnbull Inc., San Francisco

Elevator Consultant   Edgett Williams Consulting Group Inc., Mill Valley

Approximate Cost   US$ 83,000,000

Building Area   106,680 m² (including 30,480 m² of renovated facilities and
15,240 m² addition)

Photographer   Abby Sadin, San Francisco

Further Reading   Betsky Aaron: Preservation Technology: Isolated Grandeur,
Architecture Magazine, July 1997, pp. 146–152

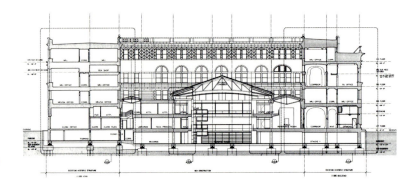

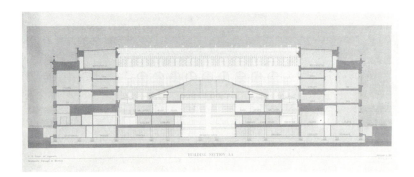

Daniel Solomon and Gary Strang Architects with Philip C. Rossington, San Francisco
Beth Israel Memorial Chapel and Garden

Houston, Texas, USA
1993–February 1997

Award   AIA Religious Art and Architecture Design Award 1998
Given by   AIA The American Institute of Architects
Prize Presentation   October 1998
Members of the Jury   John Ruble, Vienna Cobb Anderson,
  Michael Berkowicz, Andrea Clark Brown, Michael Underhill
Design Team   Daniel Solomon and Gary Strang Architects with
  Philip C. Rossington, San Francisco
Structural Engineering   Matrix Structural Engineers, Houston
Civil Engineering   Walter P. Moore and Associates, Inc, Houston
Mechanical Engineering   Design/Build
Electrical Engineering   Design/Build
Environmental Engineering   Charles Benton, San Francisco
Acoustic Engineering   Charles M. Salter Associates, Inc., San Francisco
Lighting Consultant   Auerbach + Glasow, San Francisco
Color Consultant   James Goodman, San Francisco
Landscape Architecture   Daniel Solomon and Gary Strang Architects
  with Philip C. Rossington, San Francisco
Quantity Surveying & General Contractor   W. S. Bellows
  Construction Corporation
Site Area   12,140 m²
Building Area   483 m²
Total Floor Area   483 m²
Photographer   Timothy Hursley, Little Rock, Arkansas, USA;
  Gary Strang, San Francisco, California, USA

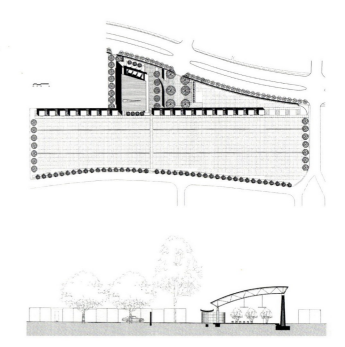

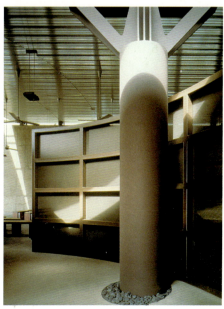

Studio E Architects, San Diego
Orange Place Cooperative
Escondido, California, USA

Award   AIA National Honor Award for Architecture 1998
Given by   AIA The American Institute of Architects
Prize Presentation   May/16/1998
Members of the Jury   Mark Simon, Walter F. Chatham, Susan F. Child, Bruce A. Eckfeldt, Michael Quinn, Adele Naude-Santos, Peter L. Schaudt, Scott A. Welch, Allison Williams, Robert Ziegelman
Design Team   Eric Naslund (Design Lead), John Sheehan, Brad Burke
Structural Engineering   Mesri Engineering
Civil Engineering   North County Engineering
Mechanical Engineering   Harington Engineering
Interior Design   Studio E Architects
Landscape Architecture   Andrew Spurlock, Martin Poirier, San Diego
Approximate Cost   US$ 2,200,000
Site Area   7,688 m²
Total Floor Area   3,000 m²
Photographer   Jim Brady
Further Reading   Architectural Record (US), May 1998

TAMS Consultants Inc. Architects, Engineers & Planners (Joint Venture of TAMS/URS/Gannett Fleming), Boston; Wallace, Floyd, Associates, Inc. & Stull and Lee, Inc. (Joint Venture of Bechtell and Parsons Brinkerhoff)
Ventilation Building/Ted Williams Tunnel

Logan International Airport, Boston, Massachusetts, USA
1990–1997

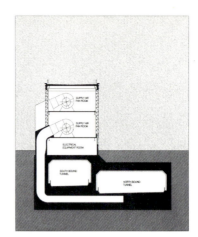 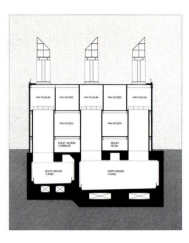

Award   AIA National Honor Award for Architecture 1998
Given by   AIA The American Institute of Architects
Prize Presentation   May/16/1998
Members of the Jury   Mark Simon, Walter F. Chatham, Susan F. Child,
   Bruce A. Eckfeldt, Michael Quinn, Adele Naude-Santos, Peter L. Schaudt,
   Scott A. Welch, Allison Williams, Robert Ziegelman
Final Design and Design Development Team   TAMS Architects, Engineers &
   Planners – Deborah Fennick, Chris Iwerks (Design Principals), David Lunny
   (Project Architect), Beth Larkin (Project Manager), Jim Armstrong, Deborah Allen,
   Herb Everett, Martha Kennan (Project Team)
Preliminary and System-Wide Design Team   Wallace, Floyd, Associates,
   Inc. – Doug McCallum (Lead Designer), Hubert Murray (Chief Architect);
   Stull & Lee Inc. – David Lee (Principal)
Structural Engineering   TAMS Architects Engineers & Planners (Final Design);
   Bechtel/Parsons Brinkerhoff (Preliminary Design)
Civil Engineering   URS (Final Design); Bechtel/Parsons Brinkerhoff
   (Preliminary Design)
Mechanical and Electrical Engineering   SAR Engineering (Final Design);
   Bechtel/Parsons Brinkerhoff (Preliminary Design); Sverdrup Civil
   (System Wide Design)
Landscape Architecture   Pat Loheed Landscape Architect (Final Design);
   Carol Johnson & Associates (Preliminary Design)
Approximate Cost   US$ 15,000,000
Site Area   3,500 m²
Building Area   9,500 m²
Photographer   Peter Vanderwarker
Further Reading   Architectural Record, February 1998

Westfourth Architecture P.C., New York
101 Cityfood Cafe

New York, N.Y., USA
July 1996 – June 1997

Award   AIA National Honor Award for Interiors 1998
Given by   AIA The American Institute of Architects
Prize Presentation   May/16/1998
Members of the Jury   Steven Goldberg, Heather Willson Cass,
   Hendrik Koning, Eva Maddox, Merry Norris
Design Team   Vladimir Arsene, Zing Lee, John Daly Bruning
Structural Engineering   Emanuel E. Necula Consulting Engineers, P.C.
Mechanical Engineering   Martin A. Huber Consulting Engineers, P.C.
Electrical Engineering   Martin A. Huber Consulting Engineers, P.C.
Lighting Consultant   Lampyridae
Approximate Cost   US$ 1,000,000
Total Floor Area   650 m²
Photographer   Lynn Massimo Photography
Further Reading   Space Architecture Art Design, March 1998, vol. 364

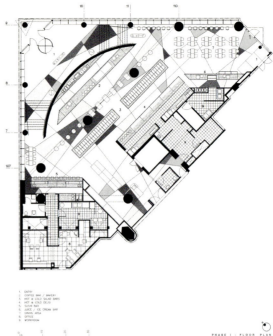

Chris Wilkinson Architects, London
South Quay Footbridge

London, United Kingdom
completed May 1997

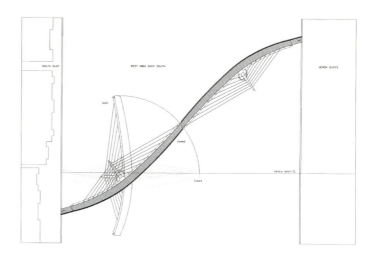

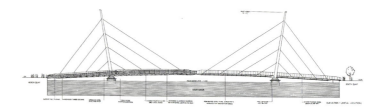

Award   AIA Award for Excellence in Design 1997
Given by   AIA The American Institute of Architects
Prize Presentation   1997
Design Team   Dominic Bettison, Keith Brownlie (Project Architect), Jim Eyre
   (Director in Charge), Chris Wilkinson
Structural Engineering   Jan Bobrowski & Partners
Mechanical Engineering   Multi BBRV (Mechanical/Hydraulic/Cables)
Life Safety Consultant   Jan Bobrowski & Partners
Quantity Surveying   Bucknall Austin PLC
Approximate Cost   £ 2,500,000
Site Area   180 m²
Photographer   Allan Williams, Susan Kay
Further Reading   L'ARCA March 1998

Williams & Dynerman Architects, Washington
The Henri Beaufour Institute

Washington, DC, USA
October 1991–February 1993

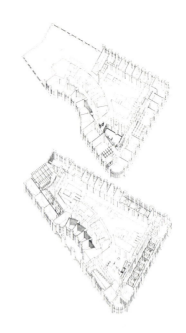

Award   AIA National Honor Award for Architecture 1997
Given by   AIA The American Institute of Architects
Prize Presentation   May/18/1997
Members of the Jury   Malcolm Holzman (Chair), F. Michael Ayles,
    Dana Cuff, Joan E. Goody, Aaron E. Johnson, Susan Henshaw Jones,
    Robert L. Thompson, Anne G. Tyng, Robert Yudell
Design Team   Alan Dynerman (Partner in Charge, Principal Designer),
    Robert Dudka (Project Architect)
Structural Engineering   Tadjer Cohen, Silver Spring
Mechanical Engineering   GHT. Arlington
Electrical Engineering   GHT. Arlington
Lighting Consultant   Williams & Dynerman Architects
Interior Design   Williams & Dynerman Architects
Approximate Cost   US$ 1,600,000
Total Floor Area   2,600 m²
Photographer   Paul Warchol

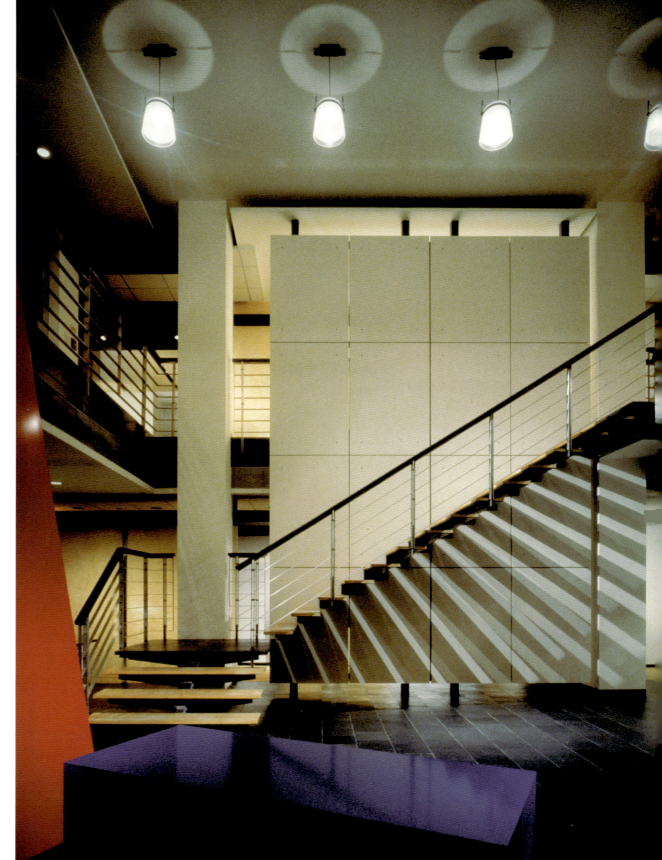

Tod Williams Billie Tsien and Associates, New York
The Neurosciences Institute

La Jolla, California, USA
1992–1995

Award   AIA National Honor Award for Architecture 1997
Given by   AIA The American Institute of Architects
Prize Presentation   May/18/1997
Members of the Jury   Malcolm Holzman (Chair), F. Michael Ayles, Dana Cuff,
   Joan E. Goody, Aaron E. Johnson, Susan Henshaw Jones, Robert L. Thompson,
   Anne G. Tyng, Robert Yudell
Design Team   David van Handel (Project Architect), Erika Hinrichs, Matthew Baird,
   Betty Chen, Chris McVoy, Peter Burns, Brett Ettinger, Yoshiko Sato, Peter Arnold,
   Martin Finio, Johannes Käferstein, Matthew Pickner, Marwan Al-Sayed, Vivian Wang
   (Project Team), Joseph Wong Design Associates (Associate Architect)
Structural Engineering   Severud Associates
Civil Engineering   RBF/Sholders and Sanford
Mechanical Engineering   Tsuchiyama, Kaino & Gibson
Electrical Engineering   Randall Lamb Associates
Consulting Engineering   Ambrosino, DePinto & Schmieder
Acoustical Consultant   Cyril M. Harris
Acoustical/AV   McKay Conant Brook
Audio Visual   Klepper Marshall King
Lighting Consultant   Randall Lamb Associates
Landscape Architecture   Burton Associates
Laboratories   AI Associates
Approximate Cost   US$ 15,000,000
Site Area   16,000 m²
Building Area   5,200 m²
Photographer   Michael Moran, Bill Timmerman, Owen McGoldrick
Further Reading   Global Architectura Document 50, May 1997

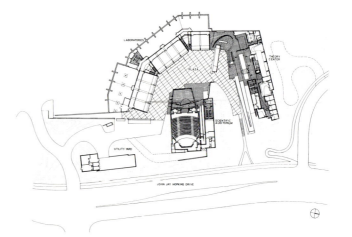

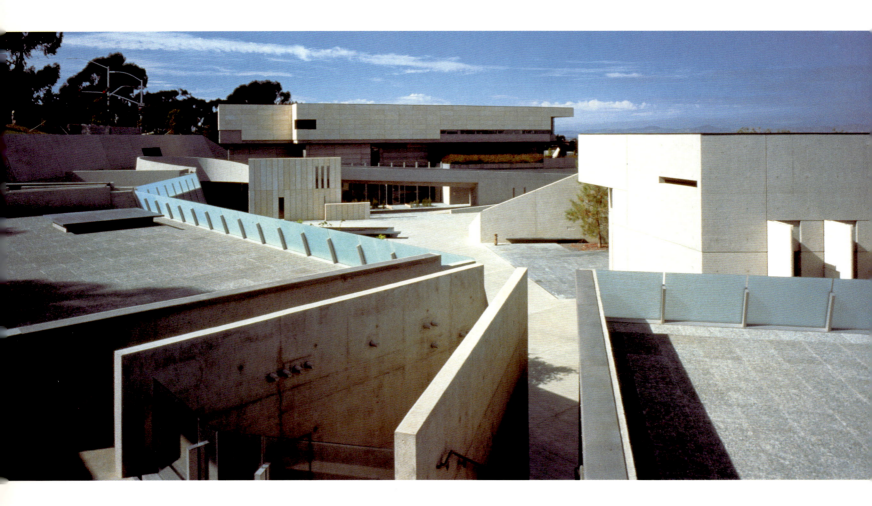

Zimmer Gunsul Frasca Partnership, Seattle
Bellevue Regional Library

Bellevue, Washington, USA
February 1991–February 1993

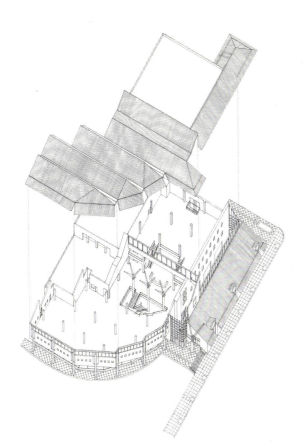

Award   AIA National Honor Award for Architecture 1997
Given by   AIA The American Institute of Architects
Prize Presentation   May/18/1997
Members of the Jury   Malcolm Holzman (Chair), F. Michael Ayles,
    Dana Cuff, Joan E. Goody, Aaron E. Johnson, Susan Henshaw Jones,
    Robert L. Thompson, Anne G. Tyng, Robert Yudell
Design Team   Robert Frasca, Ev Ruffcorn, Daniel Huberty, Stan Zintel,
    Bob Zimmerman, Bill LaPatra, Terri Johnson
Structural Engineering   KPFF Consulting Engineers
Civil Engineering   KPFF Consulting Engineers
Mechanical Engineering   Notkin Engineers
Electrical Engineering   Sparling
Acoustic Engineering   Michael R. Yantis Associates, Inc. P.S.
Air Conditioning Consultant   Notkin Engineers
Lighting Consultant   Sparling/Candela
Interior Design   Zimmer Gunsul Frasca Partnership
Landscape Architecture   Jones & Jones
Quantity Surveying   Zimmer Gunsul Frasca Partnership
Approximate Cost   US$ 11,800,000
Site Area   14,574 m²
Building Area   11,811 m²
Total Floor Area   7,509 m²
Photographer   Strode Eckert Photographic and Timothy Hursley
Further Reading   Zimmer Gunsul Frasca: Building Community

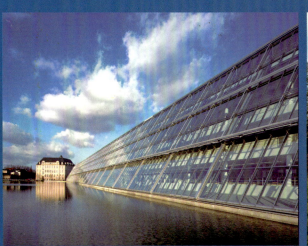

COMPREHENSIVE LISTING
OF PROJECTS

AMA 1998/99 includes awards from national associations of architects, listed country by country in alphabetical order. Within each country, the individual architects are also listed alphabetically. A number of selected projects are documented in detail, with photographs, in the first section of the book. These are indicated with a page number for cross-reference. The awards in question are the highest accolades presented by the respective national architects' associations. Where such an association does not actually grant an award itself, an equivalent award by another institution or foundation has been included on the recommendation of the national architects' association.

AUSTRALIA

Lawrence Nield and Partners Australia in Association with John Mainwaring & Associates Pty. Ltd., Noosa Heads (see p. 12)
Award Winning Building Sunshine Coast University College Library
Location Sippy Downs, Sunshine Coast, Queensland, Australia
Design and Construction Period Aug. 1995–Jan. 1997
Award Sir Zelman Cowen Award for Public Buildings
Given by RAIA The Royal Australian Institute of Architects
Further Reading Australian Architect, May/June 1997 and November/December 1997

AUSTRIA

Eduard Begusch, Vienna
Award Winning Building Das Vertikale Zweimannzelt
Design and Construction Period 1996
Award Förderungspreis für Experimentelle Tendenzen 1996 (Anerkennung)
Given by Republik Österreich Bundeskanzleramt – Staatssekretariat für Kunst

Andreas Haase, Max Huber, Killian Kada, Vienna
Award Winning Building Mikrobrigator Project in Progress
Location Havanna, Cuba
Award Förderungspreis für Experimentelle Tendenzen 1996 (Lobende Erwähnung)
Given by Republik Österreich Bundeskanzleramt – Staatssekretariat für Kunst
Further Reading Architektur und Bauforum

Benjamin Vincenz Jourdan, Vienna
Award Winning Building Chill-out-City
Location Vienna, Austria
Design and Construction Period 1996
Award Förderungspreis für Experimentelle Tendenzen 1996
Given by Republik Österreich Bundeskanzleramt – Staatssekretariat für Kunst
Further Reading 1) Architektur & Bauforum September/October 1997, pp. 9–10; 2) Klassen Katalog 1996 der MKL. A3, W. D. Prix

Elena Neururer-Theodorou, Alois Neururer, Vienna (see p. 14)
Award Winning Building Hotel Klinglhuber
Location Krems, Austria
Design and Construction Period 1994–1996
Award Staatspreis 1996 für Wirtschaftsbauten: Tourismus und Architektur
Given by Bundesministerium für wirtschaftliche Angelegenheiten
Further Reading Waechter-Böhm, Lisbeth: Neururer & Neururer. Schlichtheit währt am längsten, In: architektur aktuell 198/1996, pp. 74–78

the POOR BOYs ENTERPRISE – Harnoncourt & Haydn + Fuchs, Vienna
Award Winning Building Hirnsegel Nr. 7
Location Vienna, Austria
Design and Construction Period November 1995
Award Förderungspreis für Exp. Tendenzen 1996
Given by Republik Österreich Bundeskanzleramt – Staatssekretariat für Kunst
Further Reading Architektur & Bauforum, September/October 1997, no. 190

Margit Schwarz, Kindberg
Award Winning Building Kinderarchitektur
Location Austria
Award Förderungspreis für Experimentelle Tendenzen 1996 (Lobende Erwähnung)
Given by Republik Österreich Bundeskanzleramt – Staatssekretariat für Kunst

BELGIUM

Atelier d'architecture – Pierre Hebbelinck, Alain Richard, Liège
Award Winning Building Agence P & V – Waremme
Location Waremme, Belgium
Design and Construction Period 1994–1996
Award Euro Belgian Architectural Awards 1998 – Grand Prix d'Architecture de Belgique
Given by Arch & Life
Further Reading DOMUS, February 1997, no. 790, p. 24

Cuypers & Q – Gert Cuypers, Ilze Quaeyhaegens, Antwerp
Award Winning Building Intervention in a Bel-Étage-House
Location Antwerp, Belgium
Design and Construction Period 1992–1995
Award Euro Belgian Architectural Awards 1998 – Grand Prix d'Architecture de Belgique
Given by Arch & Life
Further Reading KNACK Weekend, no. 7, February/17/1998, Vitg.Mediaxis.Bruxelles

Philippe Jourdan, Serge Humblet, Libramont
Award Winning Building Neuf Habitations Groupées à ossature et bardage bois
Location Bastogne, Belgium
Design and Construction Period May 1995–August 1997
Award Euro Belgian Architectural Awards 1998, Catégorie Habitation Individuelle
Given by Arch & Life

Jan Tanghe (past partner of Groep Planning), Brussels – Brugge
Award Winning Building Estacade à St. Valéry-sur-Somme
Location St. Valéry-sur-Somme, France
Design and Construction Period 1992–1995
Award Euro Belgian Architectural Awards 1998 – Grand Prix d'Architecture de Belgique
Given by Arch & Life
Further Reading Groep Planning – Verweven als leidraad 1966–1996, hg. von Marc Van de Wiele, Brugge 1997

Jan Tanghe (past partner of Groep Planning), Brussels – Brugge
Award Winning Building Concert Noble
Location Brussels, Belgium
Design and Construction Period 1981–1986
Award Euro Belgian Architectural Awards 1998 – Grand Prix d'Architecture de Belgique
Given by Arch & Life
Further Reading Groep Planning – Verweven als leidraad 1966–1996, hg. von Marc Van de Wiele, Brugge 1997

Jef van Oevelen, Ekeren
Award Winning Building Row House De Wolf
Location Deurne, Antwerp, Belgium
Design and Construction Period 1994–1997

Award Euro Belgian Architectural Awards 1998, Catégorie Habitation Individuelle
Given by Arch & Life
Further Reading De Compacte Woning op prijs gesteld, Stichting Het Kunstboek

BRAZIL

Roberto Andrade, Maria Eliza Guerra
Award Winning Building Children's School
Location Uberlândia, MG, Brazil
Design and Construction Period 1992–1993
Award Prêmio VI. de Arquitetura Minas Gerais 1997
Given by IAB Instituto de Arquitetos do Brasil, Departamento Minas Gerais
Further Reading Magazine: Projeto no. 172, pp. 41–43

Nelson Fagundes Araújo
Award Winning Building Residencial Cheverny
Location Natal, Brazil
Design and Construction Period 1997
Award Prêmio I. de Arquitetura Potiguar
Given by IAB Instituto de Arquitetos do Brasil

Eduardo Barra
Award Winning Building Residência Novo Leblon
Location Rio de Janeiro, Brazil
Design and Construction Period 1996–1997
Award Prêmio Auguste François Marie Glaziou
Given by IAB Instituto de Arquitetos do Brasil

Antonio Carlos Barossi, José Oswaldo Vilela
Award Winning Building Escola EEPG Galo Branco
Location São José dos Campos, Brazil
Design and Construction Period 1996–1997
Award Prêmio III. Bienal Internacional de Arquitetura
Given by IAB Instituto de Arquitetos do Brasil

Paulo Julio Valentino Bruna, Roberto Cerqueira Cesar
Award Winning Building Ática Shopping Cultural
Location São Paulo, Brazil
Design and Construction Period 1995–1997
Award Prêmio III. Bienal Internacional de Arquitetura
Given by IAB Instituto de Arquitetos do Brasil

Angelo Bucci and Alvaro Puntoni
Award Winning Building Residence Hotel at São Sebastião
Location Juquehy Beach, São Sebastião, Brazil
Design and Construction Period 1993–1997
Award Prêmio III. Jovens de Arquitetura 1997
Given by IAB Instituto dos Arquitetos do Brasil
Further Reading Revista Projeto Design, no. 207, April 1997, Arco Editorial Ltda., São Paulo, pp. 46–52

Marieta Cardoso Maciel
Award Winning Building São Francisco de Assis Plaza
Location Belo Horizonte, Minas Gerais, Brazil
Design and Construction Period August 1989–October 1996
Award Prêmio VI. de Arquitetura Minas Gerais 1997
Given by IAB Instituto de Arquitetos do Brasil, Departamento Minas Gerais

Manoel Coelho, Marcia Keiko Ono, Flávio Monastier
Award Winning Building Manoel Coelho Arquitetura e Design – Head Office
Location Paraná, Curitiba, Brazil
Design and Construction Period December 1994
Award Prêmio III. Bienal Internacional de Arquitetura
Given by IAB Instituto de Arquitetos do Brasil

Manoel Coelho (Principal-in-Charge), Maria Nadir Carvalho, Marcia Keiko Ono
Award Winning Building Pontifícia Universidade Católica do Paraná, Central Library
Location Paraná, Curitiba, Brazil
Design and Construction Period February 1994
Award Prêmio pelo conjunto Obra Exposta
Given by IAB Instituto de Arquitetos do Brasil

Manoel Coelho, Antônio Elias Abrào, Lucas Bertoldo, Luciana Maoski
Award Winning Building Urban Street Furniture and City Signs
Location Paraná, Curitiba, Brazil
Design and Construction Period 1992–1997
Award Prêmio III. Bienal Internacional de Arquitetura
Given by IAB Instituto de Arquitetos do Brasil

Fernando Costa, Nilberto Gomes
Award Winning Building Memorial Gorée
Location Dakar, Senegal
Design and Construction Period May–August 1997
Award Prêmio I. de Arquitetura Potiguar
Given by IAB Instituto de Arquitetos do Brasil

Eduardo Dalcanale Martini
Award Winning Building Beach House
Location Camburi Beach, City of São Sebastião, State of São Paulo, Brazil
Design and Construction Period 1997 (under construction)
Award Prêmio III. Jovens de Arquitetura 1997
Given by IAB Instituto dos Arquitetos do Brasil

Giselle de Almeida Freire da Silva
Award Winning Building Television Station
Location Natal, Brazil
Design and Construction Period 1995–1996
Award Prêmio I. de Arquitetura Potiguar
Given by IAB Instituto de Arquitetos do Brasil

Henrique de Castro Reinach, Maurício Menezes Mendonça (see p. 15)
Award Winning Building Sacha's House
Location Piracaia, São Paulo, Brazil
Design and Construction Period 1995–1997
Award Prêmio IAB/SP 1996
Given by IAB Instituto de Arquitetos do Brasil, Departamento São Paulo
Further Reading Projeto/Design, August 1997, Revista de Arquitetura, Interiores e Design, Arco Editorial São Paulo

Arthur de Mattos Casas
Award Winning Building Yellow Giraffe – Restaurant
Location São Paulo, Brazil
Design and Construction Period 1993–December 1993
Award Prêmio III. Bienal Internacional de Arquitetura
Given by IAB Instituto de Arquitetos do Brasil

Valéria Soares de Melo Franco, Maria Berenice Ordones de Oliveira
Award Winning Building Imprensa Universitária, UFMG – Federal University of Minas Gerais
Location Belo Horizonte, Brazil
Design and Construction Period 1990–1992
Award Prêmio VI. de Arquitetura Minas Gerais 1997
Given by IAB Instituto de Arquitetos do Brasil, Departamento Minas Gerais

Ilzene Pereira de M. Rodrigues, Sheila Maria B. Lopes Emerenciano
Award Winning Building Table Moon
Location Natal, Nord State, Brazil
Design and Construction Period 1996
Award Prêmio I. de Arquitetura Potiguar
Given by IAB Instituto de Arquitetos do Brasil

João Diniz
Award Winning Building Residencial Gameleira
Location Belo Horizonte, Brazil
Award Prêmio VI. de Arquitetura Minas Gerais 1997
Given by IAB Instituto de Arquitetos do Brasil, Departamento Minas Gerais
Further Reading Revista Projeto no. 196, São Paulo, pp. 52–57

Geraldo Cançado Filho
Award Winning Building Agência News, Journals and Magazine's Store

Location Belo Horizonte, Minas Gerais, Brazil
Design and Construction Period 1996
Award Prêmio VI. de Arquitetura Minas Gerais 1997
Given by IAB Instituto de Arquitetos do Brasil, Departamento Minas Gerais

Aurelio Martinez Flores
Award Winning Building Gero – Restaurant
Location São Paulo, Brazil
Design and Construction Period 1993–1994
Award Prêmio III. Bienal Internacional de Arquitetura
Given by IAB Instituto de Arquitetos do Brasil

João Carlos Gaiger Ferreira, Rosane Bauer, Adriana Fleck, José Carlos Rosa, Porto Alegre
Award Winning Building Outlet Center DC Navegantes
Location Porto Alegre, Brazil
Design and Construction Period January 1994– October 1994
Award Prêmio III. Bienal Internacional de Arquitetura
Given by IAB Instituto de Arquitetos do Brasil

Gesto Arquitetura S/C Ltda. – Newton Massafumi Yamato, Tania Regina Parma
Award Winning Building Centro de Educação do Trabalhador
Location Rua Manoel da Nóbrega, Diadema, São Paulo, Brazil
Design and Construction Period 1994–1996
Award Prêmio III. Bienal Internacional de Arquitetura
Given by IAB Instituto de Arquitetos do Brasil

Carlos Alberto Maciel, Belo Horizonte
Award Winning Building Bydu Residence
Location Sete Lagoas, Brazil
Design and Construction Period November 1996 (under construction)
Award Prêmio III. Jovens de Arquitetura 1997
Given by IAB Instituto dos Arquitetos do Brasil
Further Reading Arquitetura & Urbanismo, Ano 12, October/November 1997, p. 123.

Leandro Medrano, São Paulo
Award Winning Building Residência em Indaiatuba
Location Indaiatuba, São Paulo, Brazil
Design and Construction Period 1992–1994
Award Prêmio III. Bienal Internacional de Arquitetura
Given by IAB Instituto de Arquitetos do Brasil

Issão Minami, José Arnaldo Degasperi da Cunha
Award Winning Building Cidade de Palmas no Tocantins
Location Palmas, Tocantins, Brazil
Design and Construction Period Feb. 1997–May 1997
Award Prêmio III. Bienal Internacional de Arquitetura
Given by IAB Instituto de Arquitetos do Brasil
Further Reading Jornal da USP, Ano XIII, no. 411, November/3–9, p. 10–1

Jorge Romano Netto
Award Winning Building Residential Building, Private House
Location Natal, Brazil
Award Prêmio I. de Arquitetura Potiguar
Given by IAB Instituto de Arquitetos do Brasil

NGM Architekten, Nedelykov, Granz, Moreira, Berlin
Award Winning Building Sports and Leisure Center Olvenstedter Platz
Location Magdeburg, Germany
Design and Construction Period 1996–2000
Award Prêmio III. Bienal Internacional de Arquitetura
Given by IAB Instituto de Arquitetos do Brasil

Claudia Nucci, Valério Pietraróia, Sérgio Camargo, São Paulo
Award Winning Building SA & A Comunicação e Marqueting
Location São Paulo, Brazil
Design and Construction Period 1996
Award Prêmio III. Jovens de Arquitetura 1997
Given by IAB Instituto dos Arquitetos do Brasil
Further Reading Projeto Design, no. 208, May 1997

Claudia Nucci, Valério Pietraróia, Sérgio Camargo, São Paulo
Award Winning Building Aquática Djan Madruga
Location Rio de Janeiro, Brazil
Design and Construction Period 1996–1998

Award Prêmiacao IAB/SP 1996
Given by IAB Instituto de Arquitetos do Brasil, Departamento São Paulo
Further Reading Projeto Design, no. 209, June 1997

Doris Oliveira, Evaldo Schumacher, Octacílio Rosa Ribeira, Teofilo Meditsch and Vera Maria Becker
Award Winning Building Public Market, Restoration Design and Carry out
Location Estado do Rio Grande do Sul, Brazil
Design and Construction Period 1989–1997
Award Prêmio III. Bienal Internacional de Arquitetura
Given by IAB Instituto de Arquitetos do Brasil

Paulo Henrique Paranhos (see p. 16)
Award Winning Building Espaço Cultural de Palmas
Location Palmas, Brazil
Design and Construction Period April 1994–Nov. 1996
Award Prêmio III. Jovens de Arquitetura 1997
Given by IAB Instituto de Arquitetos do Brasil
Further Reading Revista Au, no. 76, Brazil

Victor Reif
Award Winning Building Georges Hanna Khalil's Residence
Location São Paulo, Brazil
Design and Construction Period 1958–1959
Award Prêmio IAB/SP 1996
Given by IAB Instituto de Arquitetos do Brasil, Departamento São Paulo

Alessandro Rende, Rodrigo Meniconi
Award Winning Building Palacio dos Leoes
Location Uberlândia, Brazil
Design and Construction Period 1995–1996
Award Prêmio III. Bienal Internacional de Arquitetura
Given by IAB Instituto de Arquitetos do Brasil

Gregorio Repsold, Rio de Janeiro
Award Winning Building Praça dos Namorados
Location Vitória, Brazil
Design and Construction Period 1995–1996
Award Prêmio Popular Cidade de Vitória
Given by Prefeitura Municipal de Vitória
Further Reading Magazine of Architecture, no. 116 Projeto

Fernanda Cláudia Lacerda Rocha
Award Winning Building Syrup Factory Ponto do Guaraná
Location Eusébio, Ceará, Brazil
Design and Construction Period 1996–1997
Award Prêmio III. Jovens de Arquitetura 1997
Given by IAB Instituto dos Arquitetos do Brasil

Geraldo Alexandre Senra
Award Winning Building Casa Azul
Location Nova Lima, Minas Gerais, Brazil
Design and Construction Period 1989–1994
Award Prêmio VI. de Arquitetura Minas Gerais 1997
Given by IAB Instituto de Arquitetos do Brasil, Departamento Minas Gerais

Marco Aurélio Ferreira Silva, Belo Horizonte
Award Winning Building Private House
Location Belo Horizonte, Minas Gerais, Brazil
Design and Construction Period 1991–1995
Award Prêmio VI. de Arquitetura Minas Gerais 1997
Given by IAB Instituto de Arquitetos do Brasil, Departamento Minas Gerais
Further Reading Residência no São Bento; AP-Arquitetura, Design e Interiores, no. 1, April 1995

João Walter Toscano, Odiléa Setti Toscano
Location São Paulo, Brazil
Design and Construction Period 1992–1994
Award Prêmio III. Bienal Internacional de Arquitetura
Given by IAB Instituto de Arquitetos do Brasil

Julio Vieira, Carlos Eduardo Sguillaro
Award Winning Building Edifício Faria Lima Business Center
Location Avenida Faria Lima no. 1309, São Paulo, Brazil
Design and Construction Period July 1994– March 1997
Award Prêmio III. Jovens de Arquitetura 1997
Given by IAB Instituto dos Arquitetos do Brasil
Further Reading Revista Projeto no. 209 Capa e páginas 42–49

CROATIA

Hildegard Auf-Franić, Tonči Žarnic, Zagreb
Award Winning Building   Nursery and Kindergarten
Location   Zagreb, Croatia
Design and Construction Period   1994–1996
Award   1) Viktor Kovačič Award;
  2) Vladimir Nazor Award
Given by   1) Croatian Architects Association;
  2) Ministry of Culture of the Republic of Croatia
Further Reading   Architetture di confine, Triennale di
  Milano, Associazione Arte & Architettura, Udine 1997

Zoran Boševski, Boris Fiolić–Studio B & F, Zagreb
Award Winning Building   Two Apartment Buildings,
  Štampareva Street no. 32 and 34
Location   Zagreb, Croatia
Design and Construction Period   1994–1996
Award   Drago Galić Award
Given by   Croatian Architects Association
Further Reading   ČIP, Monthly Edition of the Croatian
  Architects Association, no. 11, December 1997

Penezić + Rogina, Zagreb
Award Winning Building   Bistrot Elite
Location   Zagreb, Hrvatska, Croatia
Design and Construction Period   1995–1996
Award   Bernardo Bernardi Award
Given by   Croatian Architects Association
Further Reading   Architektur Aktuell, Vienna, April 1997

Penezić + Rogina, Zagreb
Award Winning Building   Velebit Office
Location   Zagreb, Hrvatska, Croatia
Design and Construction Period   1985–1996
Award   Viktor Kovačič Award
Given by   Croatian Architects Association
Further Reading   Architektur Aktuell, Vienna, April 1997

CZECH REPUBLIC

Josef Kiszka, Barbara Potysz, Havirov
Award Winning Building   Secondary School
Location   Orlová, Czech Republic
Design and Construction Period   1993–1996
Award   Grand Prix 1996
Given by   Society of Czech Architects

**Michael Kohout, Zdeněk Jiran, František Čejka,
  Petr Stolín, Prague**
Award Winning Building   House of Assisted Living
Location   Liberec-Ruprechtice, Czech Republic
Design and Construction Period   March 1994–May 1996
Award   Grand Prix 1996
Given by   Society of Czech Architects
Further Reading   Stavba June 1996

Ivan Kroupa, Tomáš Novotný, Prague
Award Winning Building   The Interior of an Apartment
  in Prague-Radlice
Location   Prague-Radlice, Czech Republic
Design and Construction Period   1996
Award   Grand Prix 1996
Given by   Society of Czech Architects
Further Reading   ABITARE 363

DENMARK

**Herzog + Partner – Thomas Herzog, Hanns Jörg
  Schrade, Roland Schneider, Munich; BKSP
  Projektpartner GmbH, Hanover**
Representative Building   Halle 26 der Deutschen
  Messe AG
Location   Hanover, Germany
Design and Construction Period   1994–1996
Award   Den Grønne Nål 1998
Given by   DAL Danske Arkitekters Landsforbund,
  Akademisk Arkitektforening
Further Reading   Herzog Thomas, die Halle/hall/il
  padiglione 26, Prestel Verlag Munich/New York 1996

Schmidt, Hammer & Lassen A/S, Århus   (see p. 18)
Award Winning Building   Katuaq Cultural Center
  Greenland
Location   Nuuk, Greenland
Design and Construction Period   1994–1997
Award   Aereskalejdoskop 1996
Given by   DAL Danske Arkitekters Landsforbund,
  Akademisk Arkitektforening

FINLAND

Ola Laiho, Mikko Pulkkinen, Ilpo Raunio, Turku
  (see p. 20)
Representative Building   Turku Music Conservatory
Location   Turku, Finland
Design and Construction Period   1992–1994
Award   Suomi Palkinto
Given by   Valtion Rakennustaidetoimikunta
Further Reading   Glasforum 6/1995, Arkkitehti
  5–6/1995

Olavi Mäkelä, Pori
Award Winning Project   Pori City Centre Project 2000
Location   Pori, Finland
Award   SAFA prize 1997
Given by   The Finnish Association of Architects

**Suunnittelutoimisto KOKO3 Oy, Aino Brandt, Jukka
  Halminen, Helka Parkkinen, Helsinki**
Represenative Building   Gramex Façade and Light
  Construction
Location   Helsinki, Finland
Design and Construction Period   1995–1996
Award   Carin ja Erik Bryggmannin Säätiön Stipendi
Given by   Carin ja Erik Bryggmannin Säätiö

FRANCE

Joseph Almudever et Christian Lefebvre, Toulouse
  (see p. 22)
Award Winning Building   Centre Regional de la
  Propriété Forestière Auzeville
Location   Auzeville-Tolosane, France
Given by   AMO Architecture et Maîtres d'Ouvrage
Further Reading   Arca International, no. 6, Sept. 1997

Dominique Coulon, Strasbourg   (see p. 24)
Award Winning Building   Collège Pasteur
Location   Strasbourg, France
Design and Construction Period   1995–1996
Award   Prix de la Première Oeuvre
Given by   Le Moniteur

**Agence Franc – Gérard Franc, Jean-Claude
  Chauvidon, Paris**   (see p. 26)
Award Winning Building   Usine Axe
Location   Saint-Désir-de-Lisieux, France
Design and Construction Period   1992–1995
Award   Prix AMO 1996
Given by   AMO Architecture et Maîtres d'Ouvrage
Further Reading   Le Moniteur, Architecture – AMC,
  February 1997

Jean-Marc Ibos and Myrto Vitart, Paris   (see p. 28)
Award Winning Building   The Fine Arts Museum
  of Lille
Location   Lille, France
Design and Construction Period   1990–1997
Award   Prix de l'Equerre d'Argent
Given by   Le Moniteur
Further Reading   Le Moniteur A.M.C., No 82,
  September 1997, pp. 23–35

Claude Montfort, Paris
Award Winning Building   Restaurant et Locaux
  d'Enseignement Universitaires
Location   Rennes, France
Design and Construction Period   1994–1996
Award   Mention au prix de la Première Oeuvre
Given by   Le Moniteur

GERMANY

**AGH – Arnke und Häntsch, Berlin; Göken Architekt,
  Oldenburg**
Award Winning Building   Umbau und Erweiterung der
  Landschaftsbibliothek
Location   Aurich, Germany
Design and Construction Period   1993–1996
Award   BDA Preis Niedersachsen 1997
Given by   BDA Bund Deutscher Architekten
  Niedersachsen
Further Reading   db 1/1996

**Margrit Althammer + René Hochuli, Zurich,
  Switzerland**
Award Winning Building   Uhrenfabrik Corum
Location   La Chaux-de-Fonds, Switzerland
Design and Construction Period   1992–1995
Award   Constructec-Preis 1996 (Special Award)
Given by   Deutsche Messe AG with BDA Bund
  Deutscher Architekten
Further Reading   Archithese 1/1996

**Tadao Ando, Osaka, Japan, and Günter Pfeifer,
  Lörrach, Germany**   (see p. 30)
Award Winning Building   Vitra Conference Pavillon
Location   Weil am Rhein, Germany
Design and Construction Period   1989–1993
Award   Hugo-Häring-Preis 1997 des BDA Baden-
  Württemberg
Given by   BDA Bund Deutscher Architekten Baden-
  Württemberg

Architekten Linie 4, Villingen-Schwenningen
Award Winning Building   Wohngebäude Gabi und
  Matthias Mieg
Location   Mühlhausen, Germany
Design and Construction Period   March 1994–March
  1995
Award   BDA Auszeichnung guter Bauten 1996
Given by   BDA Bund Deutscher Architekten

Werner Bäuerle, Konstanz   (see p. 32)
Award Winning Building   Duplex Söhnckestrasse,
  Munich-Solln
Location   Munich, Germany
Design and Construction Period   1996–1997
Award   BDA Preis Bayern 1997
Given by   BDA Bund Deutscher Architekten Bayern

Banz + Riecks, Bochum
Award Winning Building   Erweiterung eines
  Wohnhauses
Location   Bochum, Germany
Design and Construction Period   May 1993–May 1994
Award   BDA Auszeichnung guter Bauten 1997 der
  BDA-Kreisgruppe Bochum
Given by   BDA Bund Deutscher Architekten Nordrhein-
  Westfalen (Kreisgruppe Bochum)

BauCoop Cologne – Wolfgang Felder, Cologne
  (see p. 34)
Award Winning Building   Industrial Park Nordstern
Location   Gelsenkirchen, Germany
Design and Construction Period   1994–1997
Award   Constructec-Preis 1998 (Special Award)
Given by   Deutsche Messe AG with BDA Bund
  Deutscher Architekten
Further Reading   Centrum, Jahrbuch Architektur und
  Stadt, 1997–1998

Baumschlager & Eberle, Lochau, Austria   (see p. 36)
Award Winning Building   Building for Bearing Technology
Location   Wolfurt, Austria
Design and Construction Period   Feb. 1993–Aug. 1996
Award   Constructec-Preis 1996 (Special award)
Given by   Deutsche Messe AG with BDA Bund
  Deutscher Architekten
Further Reading   Domus, October/1995

Becker Gewers Kühn & Kühn Architekten, Berlin
  (see p. 38)
Award Winning Building   Headquarters Verbundnetz
  Gas AG
Location   Leipzig, Germany
Design and Construction Period   1992–1997

Award BDA Deubau Preis 1998
Given by BDA Bund Deutscher Architekten
Further Reading Becker Gewers Kühn & Kühn
Architekten Berlin, Verlag H.M. Nelte

Heinrich Böll, Hans Krabel, Essen (see p. 40)
Award Winning Building Former Mining Zollverein
Schacht XII, Essen
Location Essen, Germany
Design and Construction Period 1991–1998
Award Constructec-Preis 1998
Given by Deutsche Messe AG with BDA Bund
Deutscher Architekten
Further Reading Detail June 1997, pp. 873 ff.

Braun & Voigt und Partner, Frankfurt am Main
(see p. 42)
Award Winning Building MG Office Building,
Duisburg-Innenhafen
Location Duisburg, Germany
Design and Construction Period Oct. 1992–Oct. 1995
Award BDA Auszeichnung guter Bauten 1997 der
BDA-Kreisgruppe Rechter Niederrhein (Anerkennung)
Given by BDA Bund Deutscher Architekten Nordrhein-
Westfalen (Kreisgruppe Rechter Niederrhein)
Further Reading Alt und Neu – Tatort Duisburg, in:
Bauwelt 3/1996; Ausgangslage: Sonderfall –
Kontorhaus, in: AIT 10/1997

Frid + Herbert Bühler, Munich
Award Winning Building Umbau und Erweiterung der
Maria-Ward-Realschule, Sporthalle
Location Neuburg a. d. Donau, Germany
Design and Construction Period 1996
Award Anerkennung BDA Preis Bayern 1997
Given by BDA Bund Deutscher Architekten Bayern

Corneliussen + Partner, Waltrop
Award Winning Building Wohnhaus in Waltrop
Location Waltrop, Germany
Design and Construction Period Jan. 1996–Dec. 1996
Award BDA Auszeichnung guter Bauten 1997 der
BDA-Kreisgruppen Recklinghausen und Gelsenkirchen
Given by BDA Bund Deutscher Architekten Nordrhein-
Westfalen (Kreisgruppen Recklinghausen und
Gelsenkirchen)

Diözesanbauamt – Karl Frey, Eichstätt
Award Winning Building Aula am Graben
Location Eichstätt, Germany
Design and Construction Period 1993–1996
Award BDA Preis Bayern 1997
Given by BDA Bund Deutscher Architekten Bayern

Diözesanbauamt – Karl Frey + Mitarbeiter, Eichstätt
(see p. 44)
Award Winning Building Extension and Conversion
of the Orbansaal
Location Ingolstadt, Germany
Design and Construction Period 1994–1996
Award Anerkennung BDA Preis Bayern 1997
Given by BDA Bund Deutscher Architekten Bayern

Dohle + Lohse, Brunswick (see p. 45)
Award Winning Building Extension and Conversion of
the Friedensschule School Center Lingen-Darme
Location Lingen, Germany
Design and Construction Period 1994–1996
Award BDA Preis Niedersachsen 1997
Given by BDA Bund Deutscher Architekten
Niedersachsen
Further Reading Architekten in Niedersachsen

**Döring + Partner – W. Döring, M. Dahmen,
E. Joeressen, Düsseldorf**
Award Winning Building Private House E+E Stampfel
Location Meerbusch, Germany
Design and Construction Period 1995–1996
Award BDA Auszeichnung guter Bauten 1997 der
BDA-Kreisgruppe Düsseldorf
Given by BDA Bund Deutscher Architekten Nordrhein-
Westfalen (Kreisgruppe Düsseldorf)
Further Reading MD, Bauwelt, Baumeister, HÄUSER

Druschke + Grosser, Düsseldorf/Duisburg
Award Winning Building Sozialer Wohnungsbau
mit 66 Einheiten
Location Duisburg, Germany
Design and Construction Period 1993–1995

Award BDA Auszeichnung guter Bauten 1997 der
BDA-Kreisgruppe Rechter Niederrhein (Anerkennung)
Given by BDA Bund Deutscher Architekten Nordrhein-
Westfalen (Kreisgruppe Rechter Niederrhein)
Further Reading Entwerfen bis ins Detail, in: Deutsches
Architektenblatt, 1/1996; Nachverdichten von Wohn-
quartieren, in: MBW-Schriftreihe 7, 6/1996; Bauen
muß nicht teuer sein, in: Architektenkammer, 10/1996

Dietrich Fink + Thomas Jocher, Munich
Award Winning Building Haus Schroth
Location Bad Tölz, Germany
Design and Construction Period July 1995–Feb. 1996
Award BDA Preis Bayern 1997
Given by BDA Bund Deutscher Architekten Bayern
Further Reading Detail 10/1995

Foster and Partners, London (see p. 46)
Award Winning Building Microelectronic Center
Location Duisburg, Germany
Design and Construction Period 1988–1996
Award BDA Auszeichnung guter Bauten 1997 der
BDA-Kreisgruppe Rechter Niederrhein (Auszeichnung)
Given by BDA Bund Deutscher Architekten Nordrhein-
Westfalen (Kreisgruppe Rechter Niederrhein)
Further Reading The Architect's Journal, July/3/1997

Friedrich und Partner, Düsseldorf (see p. 48)
Award Winning Building Headquarters of
the Stadtwerke Witten
Location Witten, Germany
Design and Construction Period 1989–1995
Award BDA Auszeichnung guter Bauten 1997 der
BDA-Kreisgruppe Bochum
Given by BDA Bund Deutscher Architekten Nordrhein-
Westfalen (Kreisgruppe Bochum)
Further Reading Friedrich, Jörg: Hauptverwaltung der
Stadtwerke Witten, hg. von Flagge, Ingeborg, 1994

**Atelier Niklas Fritschi, Benedikt Stahl and Günter
Baum, Düsseldorf**
Award Winning Building Rheinufergestaltung Altstadtufer
Location Düsseldorf, Germany
Design and Construction Period 1991–1995
Award BDA Auszeichnung guter Bauten 1997 der
BDA-Kreisgruppe Düsseldorf
Given by BDA Bund Deutscher Architekten Nordrhein-
Westfalen (Kreisgruppe Düsseldorf)
Further Reading Bauwelt Nr. 47, December/12/1997

Gruhl & Partner, Cologne (see p. 50)
Award Winning Building Schäfer House,
Meerbusch-Büderich
Location Ahornstraße, Düsseldorf, Germany
Design and Construction Period 1991–1993
Award BDA Auszeichnung guter Bauten 1997 der
BDA-Kreisgruppe Düsseldorf
Given by BDA Bund Deutscher Architekten Nordrhein-
Westfalen (Kreisgruppe Düsseldorf)

HENN Architekten Ingenieure, Munich
Award Winning Building Škoda Automobilová
A.S./Montage A-Model
Location Mladá Boleslav, Czech Republic
Design and Construction Period Feb. 1994–Sept. 1996
Award Constructec-Preis 1998 (Special Award)
Given by Deutsche Messe AG with BDA Bund
Deutscher Architekten
Further Reading HENN, Form Follows Flow, Modulare
Fabrik Škoda

Herzog & de Meuron, Basle, Switzerland (see p. 52)
Award Winning Building SBB Switch Tower 4,
Auf dem Wolf
Location Basle, Switzerland
Design and Construction Period 1989–1994
Award Constructec-Preis 1996 (Special Award)
Given by Deutsche Messe AG with BDA Bund
Deutscher Architekten

Theo Hotz, Zurich, Switzerland
Award Winning Building ABB Kraftwerke AG,
Engineering
Location Baden, Switzerland
Design and Construction Period 1992–1995
Award Constructec-Preis 1996
Given by Deutsche Messe AG with BDA Bund
Deutscher Architekten
Further Reading Baumeister, June/6/1996, p. 24

Theo Hotz, Zurich, Switzerland
Award Winning Building EMPA Eidgenössische
Materialprüfungs- und Forschungsanstalt
Location St. Gallen, Switzerland
Design and Construction Period 1988–1996
Award Constructec-Preis 1996
Given by Deutsche Messe AG with BDA Bund
Deutscher Architekten
Further Reading Hochparterre, Nr. 11, November
1996, p. 18

Theo Hotz, Zurich, Switzerland (see p. 53)
Award Winning Building Operational Facilities for
the Gasworks Public Utilities
Location Winterthur, Switzerland
Design and Construction Period February 1990–
March 1996
Award Constructec-Preis 1996
Given by Deutsche Messe AG with BDA Bund
Deutscher Architekten
Further Reading Bauwelt 43/44, November/22/1996,
p. 2494

**Architekten HPP – Hentrich, Petschnigg & Partner,
Düsseldorf**
Award Winning Building Altenwohnheim Nikolausstift
Location Wesel, Germany
Design and Construction Period 1993–1996
Award BDA Auszeichnung guter Bauten 1997
der BDA-Kreisgruppe Rechter Niederrhein
(Auszeichnung)
Given by BDA Bund Deutscher Architekten Nordrhein-
Westfalen (Kreisgruppe Rechter Niederrhein)
Further Reading Bauwelt 87/Jg. 1996, no. 34,
pp. 1900–1905; Rizzoli: HPP Buildings & Projects
1988–1998, pp. 198–205

Wilhelm Huber with Erich Kessler, Kempten
Award Winning Building Seniorenwohnanlage
Location Eichstätt, Germany
Design and Construction Period 1995–1997
Award BDA Preis Bayern 1997
Given by BDA Bund Deutscher Architekten Bayern
Further Reading Architektur Jahrbuch 1996, Hg. v.
Deutschem Architektur-Museum, Frankfurt am Main,
Annette Becker, Wilfried Wang, Prestel Munich/
New York, pp. 108–113

Ingenhoven Overdiek Kahlen + Partner, Düsseldorf
(see p. 54)
Award Winning Building Kaistrasse 16a, Offices and
Studios
Location Düsseldorf, Germany
Design and Construction Period Dec. 1994–July 1997
Award BDA Auszeichnung guter Bauten 1997 der
BDA-Kreisgruppe Düsseldorf
Given by BDA Bund Deutscher Architekten Nordrhein-
Westfalen (Kreisgruppe Düsseldorf)

Alban Janson, Sophie Wolfrum, Stuttgart
Award Winning Building Stadtgarten Böblingen
Location Böblingen, Germany
Completion Date 1990–1996
Award Hugo-Häring-Preis 1997 des BDA Baden-
Württemberg
Given by BDA Bund Deutscher Architekten Baden-
Württemberg
Further Reading Topos 22, March 1998

Jauss + Gaupp, Friedrichshafen (see p. 55)
Award Winning Building Zeppelinmuseum
Location Friedrichshafen, Germany
Design and Construction Period 1991–1996
Award Hugo-Häring-Preis 1997 des BDA Baden-
Württemberg
Given by BDA Bund Deutscher Architekten Baden-
Württemberg
Further Reading Bauwelt, 9/1996

Jauss + Gaupp, Friedrichshafen
Award Winning Building Atelierhaus Gaupp
Location Meckenbeuren, Germany
Design and Construction Period March 1994–
October 1997
Award Hugo-Häring-Preis 1997 des BDA Baden-
Württemberg
Given by BDA Bund Deutscher Architekten Baden-
Württemberg
Further Reading db, 9/1995

Kauffmann Theilig und Partner, Stuttgart
Award Winning Building   Bad Colberg Kliniken
Location   Bad Colberg, Germany
Design and Construction Period   1993–1997
Award   Thüringer Preis für Energiesparende und
   Innovative Bauten 1998 (1. Preis)
Given by   Ingenieurkammer Thüringen
Further Reading   Glas, 5/1997; Baumeister, 10/1997

Kiessler + Partner, Munich
Award Winning Building   Literaturhaus Munich
Location   Munich, Germany
Design and Construction Period   1992–1996
Award   BDA Preis Bayern 1997
Given by   BDA Bund Deutscher Architekten Bayern
Further Reading   Baumeister, 7/1997

Kiessler + Partner, Munich   (see p. 56)
Award Winning Building   Science Park Gelsenkirchen
Location   Gelsenkirchen, Germany
Design and Construction Period   1989–1995
Award   Constructec-Preis 1998 (Special Award)
Given by   Deutsche Messe AG with BDA Bund
   Deutscher Architekten
Further Reading   Bauwelt, 9/1995

**Kai-Michael Koch, Anne Panse, Andreas-Christian
   Kühn, Hanover**   (see p. 58)
Award Winning Building   Kestner Gesellschaft Hanover,
   Conversion of the former Goserieder Baths into an
   Art Gallery
Location   Hanover, Germany
Design and Construction Period   1994–1997
Award   BDA Preis Niedersachsen 1997
Given by   BDA Bund Deutscher Architekten
   Niedersachsen

Kohl & Kohl Architekten, Duisburg/Essen   (see p. 59)
Award Winning Building   Musical Theater Colosseum
Location   Essen, Germany
Design and Construction Period   1995–1996
Award   Constructec-Preis 1998 (Special Award)
Given by   Deutsche Messe AG with BDA Bund
   Deutscher Architekten
Further Reading   Bauwelt, 3/1996

Kohl & Kohl Architekten, Duisburg/Essen
Award Winning Building   Musical Theater Duisburg
Location   Duisburg, Germany
Design and Construction Period   1993–1996
Award   BDA Auszeichnung guter Bauten 1997 der
   BDA-Kreisgruppe Rechter Niederrhein (Anerkennung)
Given by   BDA Bund Deutscher Architekten Nordrhein-
   Westfalen (Kreisgruppe Rechter Niederrhein)
Further Reading   Bauwelt, 3/1996; Rheinzink
   Yearbook 1998

Andreas Kottusch, Ebersbrunn
Award Winning Building   Wohnhaus Haus Kottusch
Location   Ebersbrunn, Germany
Award   Anerkennung BDA Preis Sachsen 1995/1996
Given by   BDA Bund Deutscher Architekten Sachsen

**Arno Lederer, Jórunn Ragnarsdóttir, Marc Oei,
   Stuttgart**
Award Winning Building   EKZ Reutlingen, Lagerhalle
   mit Bürogebäude
Location   Reutlingen, Germany
Design and Construction Period   Nov. 1991–April 1994
Award   Hugo-Häring-Preis 1997 des BDA Baden-
   Württemberg
Given by   BDA Bund Deutscher Architekten Baden-
   Württemberg
Further Reading   db, 7/1994

Gerd Lindemann + Florian Thamm, Brunswick
   (see p. 60)
Award Winning Building   Theater Kleines Haus
Location   Brunswick, Germany
Design and Construction Period   1989–1996
Award   BDA Preis Niedersachsen 1997
Given by   BDA Bund Deutscher Architekten
   Niedersachsen
Further Reading   CENTRUM, Jahrbuch Architektur und
   Stadt, 1996

Günther Lipkowsky, Andreas Groth, Oberhausen
Award Winning Building   Feldscheune Landschaftspark
   Duisburg-Nord

Location   Duisburg, Germany
Design and Construction Period   1993–1995
Award   BDA Auszeichnung guter Bauten 1997 der
   BDA-Kreisgruppe Rechter Niederrhein
Given by   BDA Bund Deutscher Architekten Nordrhein-
   Westfalen (Kreisgruppe Rechter Niederrhein)
Further Reading   Architekten in NRW 1997

Mahler Günster Fuchs, Stuttgart
Award Winning Building   Trade School Karlsruhe-
   Durlach
Location   Karlsruhe-Durlach, Germany
Design and Construction Period   1990–1994
Award   Hugo-Häring-Preis 1997 des BDA Baden-
   Württemberg
Given by   BDA Bund Deutscher Architekten Baden-
   Württemberg

Andreas Meck, Munich
Award Winning Building   Lärmschutzbebauung
Location   Waldkraiburg, Germany
Design and Construction Period   Nov. 1993–April 1996
Award   BDA Preis Bayern 1997
Given by   BDA Bund Deutscher Architekten Bayern
Further Reading   Detail, 4/1997

**Hans-Jürgen Mertens, Doris Schleithoff, Bad
   Neuenahr-Ahrweiler**
Award Winning Building   Wohnhäuser Marienweg
Location   Bad Neuenahr-Ahrweiler, Germany
Design and Construction Period   1996
Award   BDA Preis Rheinland-Pfalz 1997
Given by   BDA Bund Deutscher Architekten Rheinland-
   Pfalz

Karin Meyer, Bochum
Award Winning Building   177 öffentlich geförderte
   Wohnungen, Bochum-Dahlhausen
Location   Bochum, Germany
Design and Construction Period   1993–1996
Award   BDA Auszeichnung guter Bauten 1997 der
   BDA-Kreisgruppe Bochum
Given by   BDA Bund Deutscher Architekten Nordrhein-
   Westfalen (Kreisgruppe Bochum)
Further Reading   dbz, 11/1996

Andreas Ortner, Gabriele Ortner, Graz   (see p.62)
Award Winning Building   Workshop A. & C. Wallner
Location   Scheifling, Austria
Design and Construction Period   1993–1994
Award   Constructec-Preis 1996 (Special Award)
Given by   Deutsche Messe AG with BDA Bund
   Deutscher Architekten

Dominique Perrault, Paris   (see p. 64)
Award Winning Building   Water Purification Plant
   Sagep
Location   Irry-sur-Seine, France
Design and Construction Period   1987–1993
Award   Constructec-Preis 1996 (Special Award)
Given by   Deutsche Messe AG with BDA Bund
   Deutscher Architekten
Further Reading   Techniques & Architecture, May 1994

**Herbert Pfeiffer, Christoph Ellermann + Partner,
   Lüdinghausen/Berlin**
Award Winning Building   Altenpflegeheim Marienstift
Location   Oer-Erkenschwick, Germany
Design and Construction Period   December 1991–
   October 1993
Award   BDA Auszeichnung guter Bauten 1997 der
   BDA-Kreisgruppen Recklinghausen und
   Gelsenkirchen
Given by   BDA Bund Deutscher Architekten Nordrhein-
   Westfalen (Kreisgruppen Recklinghausen und
   Gelsenkirchen)

**Herbert Pfeiffer, Christoph Ellermann + Partner,
   Lüdinghausen/Berlin**   (see p. 66)
Award Winning Building   Gallery for Architecture and
   Work
Location   Gelsenkirchen, Germany
Design and Construction Period   February 1993–
   September 1995
Award   BDA Auszeichnung guter Bauten 1997 der
   BDA-Kreisgruppen Recklinghausen und Gelsenkirchen
Given by   BDA Bund Deutscher Architekten Nordrhein-
   Westfalen (Kreisgruppen Recklinghausen und
   Gelsenkirchen)

Sauerbruch Hutton Architekten, Berlin/London
   (see p. 68)
Award Winning Building   Photonics Center
Location   Berlin, Germany
Design and Construction Period   June 1995–March 1998
Award   Constructec-Preis 1998 (Special Award)
Given by   Deutsche Messe AG with BDA Bund
   Deutscher Architekten

Hartwig N. Schneider, Stuttgart   (see p. 70)
Award Winning Building   Kindergarten Lange Weiden
Location   Winnenden, Germany
Design and Construction Period   1994–1995
Award   Hugo-Häring-Preis 1997 des BDA Baden-
   Württemberg
Given by   BDA Bund Deutscher Architekten Baden-
   Württemberg

Erich Schneider-Wessling, Cologne
Award Winning Building   Neubau Deutsche
   Bundesstiftung Umwelt
Location   Osnabrück, Germany
Design and Construction Period   1991–1995
Award   BDA Preis Niedersachsen 1997
Given by   BDA Bund Deutscher Architekten
   Niedersachsen

**Schulitz + Partner – Helmut C. Schulitz, Stefan
   Worbes, Brunswick**   (see p. 71)
Award Winning Building   IAM Institute for Applied
   Microelectronics
Location   Brunswick, Germany
Design and Construction Period   1992–1994
Award   Constructec-Preis 1996 (Special Award)
Given by   Deutsche Messe AG with BDA Bund
   Deutscher Architekten
Further Reading   Schulitz + Partner, Bauten + Projekte,
   in: Architectural Review, Ernst & Sohn Verlag, Berlin

**Schulitz + Partner – Helmut C. Schulitz, Stefan
   Worbes, Brunswick**
Award Winning Building   Haus Günther
Location   Sottrum/Fährhof, Germany
Design and Construction Period   1995–1996
Award   MSH Preis für Architektur
Given by   Mannesmann GmbH

Schuster Architekten, Düsseldorf   (see p. 72)
Award Winning Building   School Building Realschule
   Voerde
Location   Voerde, Germany
Design and Construction Period   Nov. 1994–May 1996
Award   BDA Auszeichnung guter Bauten 1997 der
   BDA-Kreisgruppe Rechter Niederrhein
Given by   BDA Bund Deutscher Architekten Nordrhein-
   Westfalen (Kreisgruppe Rechter Niederrhein)
Further Reading   Bauwelt, 28/1996; Detail 4/1997

Steidle + Partner, Munich   (see p. 73)
Award Winning Building   Wacker-Haus, Office and
   Residential Building of the Pensionskasse der
   Wacker-Chemie
Location   Prinzregentenstraße, Munich, Germany
Design and Construction Period   1992–1997
Award   Deutscher Städtebaupreis
Given by   BDA Bund Deutscher Architekten

Fred-Jürgen Störmer, Wesel
Award Winning Building   Architekturbüro Störmer
Location   Wesel, Germany
Design and Construction Period   1994
Award   BDA Auszeichnung guter Bauten 1997 der
   BDA-Kreisgruppe Rechter Niederrhein (Auszeichnung)
Given by   BDA Bund Deutscher Architekten Nordrhein-
   Westfalen (Kreisgruppe Rechter Niederrhein)
Further Reading   AIT

Peter Stürzebecher, Hamburg/Berlin   (see p. 74)
Award Winning Building   T-House
Location   Gleisweiler, Germany
Design and Construction Period   1989–1990
Award   BDA Preis Rheinland-Pfalz 1997
Given by   BDA Bund Deutscher Architekten Rheinland-
   Pfalz
Further Reading   Bauwelt; Technique Architecture

Hans-Busso von Busse, Munich/Dortmund
Award Winning Building   Klosterkirche – Ökumenische
   Stiftung Frenswegen

Location   Nordhorn, Germany
Design and Construction Period   1989–1996
Award   1) BDA-Preis Niedersachsen 1997; 2)
   Auszeichnung zum Deutschen Architekturpreis 1997
Given by   1) BDA Bund Deutscher Architekten; 2)
   Bundesarchitektenkammer
Further Reading   von Busse, Hans-Busso: Gedanken
   zum Raum – Wege zur Form, Karl-Krämer-Verlag,
   Stuttgart/Zurich

Hans-Busso von Busse, Eberhard C. Klapp, Essen
(see p. 76)
Award Winning Building   Witten House
Location   Witten, Germany
Design and Construction Period   1990–1996
Award   1) Grand Prix Rhénan d'Architecture 1997
   (1ère mention); 2) BDA Auszeichnung guter Bauten
   1997 der BDA-Kreisgruppe Bochum
Given by   1) BDA Bund Deutscher Architekten
   Rheinland-Pfalz, BNA Bond van Nederlandse
   Architekten, Conseil National de l'Ordre des
   Architectes, BSA; 2) BDA Bund Deutscher
   Architekten Nordrhein-Westfalen (Kreisgruppe
   Bochum)

von Gerkan, Marg & Partner, Hamburg   (see p. 78)
Award Winning Building   Galeria Duisburg
Location   Duisburg, Germany
Design and Construction Period   1989–1994
Award   BDA Auszeichnung guter Bauten 1997 der
   BDA-Kreisgruppe Rechter Niederrhein (Anerkennung)
Given by   BDA Bund Deutscher Architekten Nordrhein-
   Westfalen (Kreisgruppe Rechter Niederrhein)
Further Reading   von Gerkan, Marg und Partner,
   Architecture 1991–1995

Walter von Lom + Partner, Cologne
Award Winning Building   Europäisches Bildungs-,
   Forschungs- und Informationszentrum
Location   Bochum-Springorum, Germany
Design and Construction Period   1992–1997
Award   BDA Auszeichnung guter Bauten 1997 der
   BDA-Kreisgruppe Bochum
Given by   BDA Bund Deutscher Architekten Nordrhein-
   Westfalen (Kreisgruppe Bochum)

**Peter C. von Seidlein, Horst Fischer, Egon Konrad,
Stephan Röhrl, Munich**
Award Winning Building   Commercial-Residential
   Building, Hildegardstrasse
Location   Munich, Germany
Design and Construction Period   1992–1996
Award   BDA Preis Bayern 1997
Given by   BDA Bund Deutscher Architekten Bayern
Further Reading   Baumeister, 7/1997

**Zach + Zünd Architekten – Gundula Zach, Michel
Zünd, Zurich/Stuttgart**   (see p. 80)
Award Winning Building   Haus Götz, Commercial
   Building at the Lake
Location   Böblingen, Germany
Design and Construction Period   Jan. 1993–March 1996
Award   Hugo-Häring-Preis 1997 des BDA Baden-
   Württemberg
Given by   BDA Bund Deutscher Architekten Baden-
   Württemberg
Further Reading   Architektur Aktuell, Wien 195/1996

**Günter Zamp Kelp and Julius Krauss, Arno
Brandlhuber, Düsseldorf**   (see p. 82)
Award Winning Building   Neanderthal Museum
Location   Mettmann, Germany
Design and Construction Period   Aug. 1993–Oct. 1996
Award   BDA Auszeichnung guter Bauten 1997 der
   BDA-Kreisgruppe Düsseldorf
Given by   BDA Bund Deutscher Architekten Nordrhein-
   Westfalen (Kreisgruppe Düsseldorf)
Further Reading   DAM Architektur Jahrbuch 1997,
   Prestel Verlag Munich/New York, pp.136–141; SD
   9710 Tokyo; DOMUS 789/1997

HONG KONG

Simon Kwan & Associates Ltd., Hong Kong
Award Winning Building   Jockey Club Environmental
   Building

Location   Hong Kong
Design and Construction Period   Dec. 1992–Sept. 1996
Award   Certificate of Merit 1997
Given by   HKIA The Hong Kong Institute of Architects
Further Reading   Building Journal Hong Kong China,
   September 1996

P & T Architects and Engineers Ltd., Hong Kong
(see p. 84)
Award Winning Building   City Tower
Location   Hong Kong
Design and Construction Period   1995–1997
Award   Certificate of Merit 1997
Given by   HKIA The Hong Kong Institute of Architects
Further Reading   A/U Interior, Architecture and Urbanism

HUNGARY

Péter Lenzsér, Mosonmagyaróvár
Award Winning Building   Ujhelyi Imre Primary School
Location   Mosonmagyaróvár, Hungary
Design and Construction Period   June 1994–
   September 1996
Award   Pro Architectura Prize
Given by   Association of Hungarian Architects

Péter Mátrai, Budapest
Award Winning Building   Katona Jószef County Library
Location   Kecsicemét, Hungary
Design and Construction Period   1986–1996
Award   YBL Prize
Given by   Association of Hungarian Architects
Further Reading   Hungarian Architecture Today 1997/1,
   pp. 12–37

Margit Pelényi, Pécs
Award Winning Building   Mortuary/Ravatalozó
Location   Szentlörinc, Hungary
Design and Construction Period   1993–1994
Award   Pro Architectura Prize
Given by   Association of Hungarian Architects
Further Reading   Újmagyar Épitömü – Vészet, 1997/1

László Szász, Erzsébet Hajnády, Pécs   (see p. 85)
Award Winning Building   Glaxo Wellcome
   Headquarters and Warehouse – Packaging Building
Location   Törökbálint, Hungary
Design and Construction Period   May 1994–
   September 1996
Award   Pro Architectura Prize
Given by   Association of Hungarian Architects
Further Reading   ÁTRIUM Magazin, 1998/1

ICELAND

Studio Granda, Reykjavik
Award Winning Building   The Supreme Court of
   Iceland
Location   Reykjavík, Iceland
Design and Construction Period   1993–1996
Award   DV Menningarverðlaun Fyrir Byggingarlist 1997
Given by   Dagblaðið – Visir
Further Reading   Architecture, July 1997,
   Barreneche R. A.

INDONESIA

Encona Engineering Inc., Jakarta
Award Winning Building   Surabaya PDAM Office
Location   Surabaya, East Java, Indonesia
Design and Construction Period   1989–1992
Award   Karya Arsitektur 1996
Given by   IAI Ikatan Arsitek Indonesia (Indonesian
   Institute of Architects)

Sonny Sutanto & Mira Susanty, Jakarta
Award Winning Building   Sutanto Family House
Location   Jakarta, Indonesia
Design and Construction Period   1993–1994
Award   Penghargaan Ikatan Arsitek Indonesia (IAI Award)

Given by   IAI Ikatan Arsitek Indonesia (Indonesian
   Institute of Architects)
Further Reading   Laras – Dewi (Indonesian Publication)

IRELAND

M.V. Cullinan – NBA, Dublin
Award Winning Building   St. Peter's Port
Location   Athlone, Ireland
Design and Construction Period   1991–1993
Award   RIAI Triennial Silver Medal for Housing
   1991–1992–1993 (Winner)
Given by   RIAI The Royal Institute of Architects of
   Ireland
Further Reading   AAI Awards 1994

**de Blacam and Meagher Architects + Boyd Barrett
Murphy O'Connor Architects, Dublin**
Award Winning Building   Library, Cork Institute of
   Technology
Location   Cork, Ireland
Design and Construction Period   1992–1995
Award   RIAI Triennial Gold Medal 1992–1993–1994
   (Commended)
Given by   RIAI The Royal Institute of Architects of
   Ireland
Further Reading   Detail Magazine, Oct./Nov.1996

O'Donnell & Tuomey, Dublin   (see p. 86)
Award Winning Building   Blackwood Golf Centre
Location   Near Bangor, Co. Down, Northern Ireland
Design and Construction Period   1992–1994
Award   RIAI Triennial Gold Medal 1992–1993–1994
   (Commended)
Given by   RIAI The Royal Institute of Architects of
   Ireland
Further Reading   Domus 781, April 1996

**The Office of Public Works Architectural Services,
Dublin**
Award Winning Building   Ceide Fields Visitor Centre
Location   Ballycastle, Ballina, Co. Mayo., Ireland
Design and Construction Period   1990–1993
Award   RIAI Triennial Gold Medal 1992–1993–1994
   (Winner)
Given by   RIAI The Royal Institute of Architects of
   Ireland
Further Reading   The Architects Journal,
   December/15–22/1993

Scott Tallon Walker Architects, Dublin
Award Winning Building   Teilifis Na Gaeilge
Location   Baile Na H-Abhainn, Co. Galway, Ireland
Design and Construction Period   May 1995–
   October 1996
Award   RIAI Regional Award
Given by   RIAI The Royal Institute of Architects of
   Ireland
Further Reading   Irish Architect, Dec./Jan. 1997

Scott Tallon Walker Architects, Dublin
Award Winning Building   Dublin Corporation, Civic
   Offices, Phase 2, Wood Quay
Location   Dublin, Ireland
Design and Construction Period   Sept. 1992–July 1994
Award   RIAI Triennial Gold Medal 1992–1993–1994
   (Commended)
Given by   The Royal Institute of Architects of Ireland
Given by   RIAI The Royal Institute of Architects of
   Ireland
Further Reading   Town and Gown, in: World
   Architecture, Issue no. 40

JAMAICA

Ann Hodges with Victor Haye, Kiva Small, Kingston
Award Winning Building   Strawberry Hill Hotel
Location   Irish Town, Jamaica
Design and Construction Period   1990–1995
Award   Governor General's Award
Given by   The Jamaican Institute of Architects
Further Reading   Archivos De Arquitectura Antillana –
   Ano 3 #, January/6/1998

JAPAN

Shigeru Ban, Tokyo (see p. 88)
Award Winning Building Paper Church
Location Takatori, Hyogo, Japan
Design and Construction Period March 1995–September 1995
Award JIA Prize for the Best Young Architect of the Year 1997
Given by JIA The Japan Institute of Architects
Further Reading GG portfolio/Shigeru Ban issued by GG, Spanish Publisher

Akira Sakamoto, Osaka (see p. 90)
Award Winning Building Hakuei Residence
Location Osaka, Japan
Design and Construction Period June 1995–Aug. 1996
Award JIA Prize for the Best Young Architect of the Year 1997
Given by JIA The Japan Institute of Architects

Kazuo Watabe, Tokyo (see p. 92)
Award Winning Building Kikyo Extended Care Facility Affiliated to OTA General Hospital
Location Koriyama, Fukushima Prefecture, Japan
Design and Construction Period June 1994–May 1996
Award JIA Prize for the Best Young Architect of the Year 1997
Given by JIA The Japan Institute of Architects

KOREA

Young Baek Min, Seoul
Award Winning Building An Epitome of Sungbookville House
Location Sungbook Dong, Sungbook ku, Seoul, Korea
Design and Construction Period March 1993–Oct. 1997
Award 20th Korean Institute of Architects Prize 1998
Given by Korean Institute of Architects
Further Reading PLUS Magazine, Korea

Sea-Young Chang (dead), Seoul
Award Winning Building Glassforum
Location 229 Wonseo-Dong, Chongno-Ku, Seoul, Korea
Design and Construction Period 1996–1997
Award 20th Korean Institute of Architects Prize 1998
Given by Korean Institute of Architects

Du-Nam Choi, Seoul (see p. 94)
Award Winning Building Gallery SamTuh
Location ChoungDamDong, KangNamKu, Seoul, Korea
Design and Construction Period July 1994–August 1997
Award 20th Korean Institute of Architects Prize 1998
Given by Korean Institute of Architects
Further Reading Korean Architects, October 1997

Nak Jung Kim – Jung Won Architects, Consultants & Engineers Co., Ltd., Seoul (see p. 96)
Award Winning Building Cine Plus Complex
Location Sinsa-Dong, Seoul, Korea
Design and Construction Period August 1995–December 1997
Award 20th Korean Institute of Architects Prize 1998
Given by Korean Institute of Architects

Hchioh Sang Seung, Seoul
Award Winning Building Culture & Space
Location Korea
Design and Construction Period January 1994–November 1996
Award 20th Korean Institute of Architects Prize 1998
Given by Korean Institute of Architects

Kim Won, Architects' Group Forum, Seoul
Award Winning Building Kwang-Ju Catholic University
Location Na-ju-gun, South Cholla Province, South Korea
Design and Construction Period November 1993–December 1997
Award 20th Korean Institute of Architects Prize 1998
Given by Korean Institute of Architects

Kerl Yoo, Seoul
Award Winning Building Milral School
Location Seoul, Korea
Completed August 1995–July 1997
Award 20th Korean Institute of Architects Prize 1998
Given by Korean Institute of Architects
Further Reading Korean Architects 157

LATVIA

Edgars Berzins
Award Winning Building Reception Hall of the Social Insurance Board of Riga City Ziemelu District
Location Riga, Latvia
Design and Construction Period 1995–1997
Award Prize for the Best New Building with the Use of Innovative Materials 1997
Given by The Latvia Association of Architects

MALAYSIA

T. R. Hamzah & Yeang Sdn. Bhd., Selangor (see p. 97)
Award Winning Building Central Plaza
Location 34 Jalan Sultan Ismail, Kuala Lumpur, Malaysia
Design and Construction Period 1992–1996
Award PAM Architecture Award 1997 (Commercial Category)
Given by PAM Pertubuhan Akitek Malaysia
Further Reading Architectural Review, September 1996

Joseph Khoo – Tensegrity, Kuala Lumpur
Award Winning Building Office for an Architect
Location Kuala Lumpur, Malaysia
Award PAM Architecture Award 1997 (Interior Design Category)
Given by PAM Pertubuhan Akitek Malaysia
Further Reading Architecture Malaysia, Vol. 9, no. 6, 1997

THE NETHERLANDS

Claus en Kaan Architecten, Amsterdam (see p. 98)
Award Winning Building Binnen Wieringerstraat
Location Amsterdam, The Netherlands
Design and Construction Period 1990–1995
Award Grand Prix Rhénan d'Architecture 1997
Given by BNA Bond van Nederlandse Architekten, BDA Bund Deutscher Architekten Rheinland-Pfalz, Conseil National de l'Ordre des Architectes, BSA
Further Reading A + U April 1996

Oosterhuis Associates, Rotterdam (see p. 100)
Award Winning Building Garbage Transfer Station – Elhorst/Vloedbelt
Location Zenderen, The Netherlands
Design and Construction Period 1993–1995
Award Océ/BNA Prize for Industrial Architecture 1996
Given by BNA Bond van Nederlandse Architekten
Further Reading De architect, December 1995, pp. 36–41, ISSN 0044–8621

NORWAY

Sverre Fehn, Oslo (see p. 102)
Award Winning Building The Aukrust Centre
Location Alvdal, Norway
Design and Construction Period 1992–1996
Award Statens Byggeskikkpris 1997
Given by Norske Arkitekters Landforbund

Architect Gunnarsjaa + Kolstad AS, Oslo
Award Winning Building Ibsenkvartalet
Location Oslo, Norway
Design and Construction Period 1993–1997
Award 1) Statens Byggeskikkpris 1997; 2) Sundts Premie 1995–1996
Given by Norske Arkitekters Landforbund
Further Reading Byggekunst no. 2, 1998

PANAMA

Edwin Brown C., Panama
Award Winning Building Ashkenazi Residence
Location Panama City, Republic of Panama
Design and Construction Period 1994–1996
Award Mejores Obras de Arquitectura 1997
Given by SPIA Sociedad Panameña de Ingenieros y Arquitectos
Further Reading Mejoras Obras de Arquitectura del Ano, Panama, August 1997

Edwin Brown C. & Linet Vanesa de Brown, Panama
Award Winning Building Condominio Vista Tower
Location Panama City, Republic of Panama
Design and Construction Period 1994–1996
Award Mejores Obras de Arquitectura 1997
Given by SPIA Sociedad Panameña de Ingenieros y Arquitectos
Further Reading Mejoras Obras de Arquitectura del Ano, Panama, August 1997

Edwin Brown C. & Linet Vanesa de Brown, Panama
Award Winning Building Condominio Los Delfines
Location Panama City, Republic of Panama
Design and Construction Period 1994–1996
Award Mejores Obras de Arquitectura 1997
Given by SPIA Sociedad Panameña de Ingenieros y Arquitectos
Further Reading Architectural Design, Multiunit Housing, Links International, 1997

Gustavo Dahlgren, Arsenio Mirones, Panama
Award Winning Building Remodelación Oficinas Adrian Resources Ltd.
Location Panama City, Republic of Panama
Design and Construction Period June 1995–May 1996
Award Mejores Obras de Arquitectura 1996
Given by SPIA Sociedad Panameña de Ingenieros y Arquitectos

POLAND

1) Andrzej Kiciński, Warsaw; 2) Andrzej Kiciński, Piotr Hardecki, Tomasz Napieralski, Warsaw
Award Winning Building The Grey Villa, Headquarter of Warsaw University
Location Warsaw, Poland
Design and Construction Period 1994–1996
Award Nagroda Honorowa SARP 1997
Given by SARP Stowarzyszenie Architektów Polskich
Further Reading Architektura 6 (33), 1997

PUERTO RICO

CMA Architects & Engineers – Pedro M. Cardona Roig, Marie Louise Fiedler Damiani AIT, San Juan
Award Winning Building Guillermo Esteves & San Antonio Bridges
Location San Juan, Puerto Rico
Design and Construction Period 1996–2001
Award Mención Honorífica
Given by Colegio de Arquitectos de Puerto Rico
Further Reading El Vocero de Puerto Rico (Newspaper), Vol. 8, Num. 8182 Dic. 9, 1997

Elio S. Martínez – Joffre, San Juan
Award Winning Building Iglesia San Miguel Arcángel
Location Bayamón, Puerto Rico
Design and Construction Period 1980–1994
Award El Prêmio Nacional de Arquitectura
Given by El Colegio de Arquitectos de Puerto Rico

ROMANIA

Florian Stanciu, Iulia Stanciu, Bucharest
Award Winning Building Orthodox Cemetery Chapel
Location Chiajna S.A.I., Romania
Design and Construction Period May 1996–not finished
Award Biannual Architecture Competition 1996 (2. Prize)

Given by   UAR Uniunea Arhitect din Romania (Union of Romanian Architects)
Further Reading   Arhitext Design, no. 12/1996, pp. 32, 42

Westfourth Architecture P.C., New York
Award Winning Building   Mindbank Headquarters
Location   Bucharest, Romania
Design and Construction Period   1994–1998
Award   Biannual Architecture Competition 1998
Given by   UAR Uniunea Arhitect din Romania (Union of Romanian Architects)
Further Reading   L'Arca Edizioni, Westfourth Architecture New York Calls Bucharest

RUSSIA

E.N. Pestov, A.E. Kharitonov, I.N. Goltsev, S.G. Popov, Nizhni Novgorod
Award Winning Building   Bank Building on Malaya Pokrovskaya Street
Location   Nizhni Novgorod, Russia
Design and Construction Period   1993–1995
Award   Architecture 1996 – 4th Russian Festival (Winner)
Given by   Union of Architects of Russia

E.N. Pestov, A.E. Kharitonov, I.N. Goltsev, S.G. Popov, Nizhni Novgorod
Award Winning Building   Office Building on Frunze Street
Location   Nizhni Novgorod, Russia
Design and Construction Period   1993–1995
Award   Architecture 1996 – 4th Russian Festival (Winner)
Given by   Union of Architects of Russia

E.N. Pestov, A.E. Kharitonov, A.E. Zelyaev, S.G. Popov, Nizhni Novgorod
Award Winning Building   Apartment House on Studyenaya Street
Location   Nizhni Novgorod, Russia
Design and Construction Period   1994–1996
Award   Architecture 1996 – 4th Russian Festival (Winner)
Given by   Union of Architects of Russia

E.N. Pestov, A.E. Kharitonov, A.I. Zelyaev, S.G. Popov, Nizhni Novgorod
Award Winning Building   Apartment House on Ulyanov Street
Location   Nizhni Novgorod, Russia
Design and Construction Period   1994–1996
Award   Architecture 1996 – 4th Russian Festival (Winner)
Given by   Union of Architects of Russia

SLOVAKIA

Peter Abonyi, Martin Bištăn, Ruzomberok
Award Winning Building   Church of the Sacred Heart of Jesus in Lomná
Location   Lomná, Slovakia
Design and Construction Period   1992–1997
Award   The Dusan Jurkovic Prize
Given by   Spolok Architektov Slovenska
Further Reading   Projekt, 1/1998

Ján Bahna, Igor Palčo, Lumbomír Závodný, Milŏs Juráni, Bratislava
Award Winning Building   VUB Bank Head Office
Location   Bratislava, Slovakia
Design and Construction Period   1995–1997
Award   The Dusan Jurkovic Prize

SOUTH AFRICA

Derick de Bruyn Architect, Den Hague
Award Winning Building   House Mabet – Double Residential
Location   Waterkloof, Pretoria, South Africa

Design and Construction Period   1995–1997
Award   SAIA Award of Merit 1997
Given by   SAIA South African Institute of Architects
Further Reading   Architecture SA, May/June 1997

Heather Dodd, Linden
Award Winning Building   Cactusland
Location   Johannesburg, South Africa
Design and Construction Period   1992–1997
Award   SAIA Award of Merit 1997
Given by   SAIA South African Institute of Architects
Further Reading   South African Architect, Feb. 1998

Gapp Architects and Urban Designers, Johannesburg   (see p. 104)
Award Winning Building   Park Hyatt Hotel
Location   Johannesburg , South Africa
Design and Construction Period   1993–1996
Award   SAIA Award of Merit 1997
Given by   SAIA South African Institute of Architects
Further Reading   South African Architect, Planning

Ronald Hicks Architects, Port Elizabeth
Award Winning Building   House Holmes
Location   Port Elizabeth, South Africa
Design and Construction Period   Jan. 1995–March 1996
Award   SAIA Award of Merit 1997
Given by   SAIA South African Institute of Architects
Further Reading   South African Architectural Digest

KrugerRoos Architects and Urban Designers, Vlaeberg
Award Winning Building   Southwinds, A Retreat on the Klein River
Location   Hermanns, South Africa
Design and Construction Period   March 1994–Dec. 1996
Award   SAIA Award of Merit 1997
Given by   SAIA South African Institute of Architects

Louw Apostolellis Bergenthuin, Sandton   (see p. 106)
Award Winning Building   Siemens Park Phase 1
Location   Midrand, South Africa
Design and Construction Period   1994–1996
Award   SAIA Award of Merit 1997
Given by   SAIA South African Institute of Architects
Further Reading   SA Architect & Builder

Karen Mailer, Johannesburg
Award Winning Building   Highveld House
Location   South Africa
Design and Construction Period   Sept. 1995–Dec. 1996
Award   SAIA Award of Merit 1997
Given by   SAIA South African Institute of Architects
Further Reading   South African Architect, Planning, Style

Meyer Pienaar, Bentel Abramson and Gapp, Johannesburg   (see p. 108)
Award Winning Building   Sandton Square
Location   Sandton, South Africa
Design and Construction Period   1993–1996
Award   SAIA Award of Merit 1997
Given by   SAIA South African Institute of Architects
Further Reading   Architecture SA, October 1996

Myles Pugh Sherlock Murray, Pinetown
Award Winning Building   Church Auditorium & Facilities for Victory Faith Centre
Location   Pinetown, Natal, South Africa
Design and Construction Period   Oct. 1994–Sept. 1995
Award   SAIA Award of Merit 1997
Given by   SAIA South African Institute of Architects
Further Reading   South African Architect, Feb. 1998

Alfio Torrisi Architects, Saxonwold   (see p. 109)
Award Winning Building   The Pharmaceutical Society of Southern Africa
Location   Melrose, Johannesburg, South Africa
Design and Construction Period   April 1996–Feb. 1997
Award   SAIA Award of Merit 1997
Given by   SAIA South African Institute of Architects
Further Reading   South African Architect

Natus & Cecilia van Rensburg Architects, Nelspruit
Award Winning Building   Residence van Rensburg
Location   Nelspruit, Mpumalanga, South Africa
Design and Construction Period   1993–1996
Award   SAIA Award of Merit 1997
Given by   SAIA South African Institute of Architects
Further Reading   SA Architect

Jane Visser, Mark Thomas Architects, Vlaeberg
Award Winning Building   Beach House, Philipskraal
Location   Betty's Bay, South Africa
Design and Construction Period   1995–1996
Award   SAIA Award of Merit 1997
Given by   SAIA South African Institute of Architects
Further Reading   South African Architectural Digest 1997, Vol. 2, Conservation and Appropiate Design Responses

Stephanie Volpe in Association with Stephen Whitehead, Port Elizabeth
Award Winning Building   House Roberts
Location   Canon Rocks, Eastern Cape, South Africa
Design and Construction Period   1994–1995
Award   SAIA Award of Merit 1997
Given by   SAIA South African Institute of Architects
Further Reading   South African Architect, February 1998, p. 21

SPAIN

Manuel de las Casas, Madrid
Award Winning Building   198 Social Housing Units in Alcobendas (First Prize)
Location   Alcobendas, Madrid, Spain
Design and Construction Period   1993–1997
Award   IV Bienal de Arquitectura Española
Given by   Consejo Superior de los Colegios de Arquitectos de España; Ministerio de Fomento; Universidad Internacional Menéndez y Pelayo; Universidad de Alcalá
Further Reading   Edificios multi-residenciales, Edita Arco, S.A. Barcelona, pp. 168–179

Foster and Partners, London   (see p. 110)
Award Winning Building   Bilbao Metro
Location   Bilbao, Spain
Design and Construction Period   1987–1995
Award   III Prêmio Manuel de la Dehesa (Finalista)
Given by   Consejo Superior de los Colegios de Arquitectos de España
Further Reading   Architectural Review, May 1997

Maria Fraile, Javier Revillo, Madrid   (see p. 112)
Award Winning Building   Recinto Ferial
Location   Zamora, Spain
Design and Construction Period   1993–1996
Award   IV Bienal de Arquitectura Española 1995–1996
Given by   Consejo Superior de los Colegios de Arquitectos de España; Ministerio de Fomento; Universidad Internacional Menéndez y Pelayo; Universidad de Alcalá
Further Reading   El croquis, no. 81/82

José Manuel Gallego Jorreto, La Coruña   (see p. 114)
Award Winning Building   Museum of Fine Arts
Location   La Coruña, Galicia, Spain
Design and Construction Period   1988–1995
Award   IV Bienal de Arquitectura Española
Given by   Consejo Superior de los Colegios de Arquitectos de España; Ministerio de Fomento; Universidad Internacional Menéndez y Pelayo; Universidad de Alcalá
Further Reading   Museo de Belas Artes Da Coruña, M. Gallego, Ed. Xunta de Galicia, 1996

Javier Garcia-Solera Vera, Alfredo Paya Benedito, Alicante
Award Winning Building   Edificio de Oficinas para la Diputación Provincial
Location   Alicante, Spain
Design and Construction Period   1985–1996
Award   IV Bienal de Arquitectura Española
Given by   Consejo Superior de los Colegios de Arquitectos de España; Ministerio de Fomento; Universidad Internacional Menéndez y Pelayo; Universidad de Alcalá
Further Reading   Via Arquitectura no. 1

JJ-PP y Asociados, S.L. – Jerónimo Junquera, Estanislao Pérez Pita, Madrid   (see p. 116)
Award Winning Building   Office Building and Computing Centre for the Caja Madrid Savings Bank
Location   Las Rozas, Madrid, Spain
Design and Construction Period   April 1991–1995

Award IV Bienal de Arquitectura Española
Given by Consejo Superior de los Colegios de
   Arquitectos de España; Ministerio de Fomento;
   Universidad Internacional Menéndez y Pelayo;
   Universidad de Alcalá
Further Reading Bauwelt no. 31/32, Stuttgart 1996

Josep Lliñás Carmona, Barcelona (see p. 118)
Award Winning Building Instituto de Enseñanza
   Secundaria
Location Torredembarra, Spain
Design and Construction Period 1993–1996
Award IV Bienal de Arquitectura Española
Given by Consejo Superior de los Colegios de
   Arquitectos de España; Ministerio de Fomento;
   Universidad Internacional Menéndez y Pelayo;
   Universidad de Alcalá
Further Reading Josep Llinàs, Editorial Tanaïs
   Ediciones, Sevilla, 1997, pp. 140–151

**Sol Madridejos, Juan Carlos Sancho Osinaga,
Madrid** (see p. 120)
Award Winning Building Polideportivo Valvanera
Location San Sebastian de los Reyes, Madrid, Spain
Design and Construction Period 1991–1996
Award IV Bienal de Arquitectura Española
Given by Consejo Superior de los Colegios de
   Arquitectos de España; Ministerio de Fomento;
   Universidad Internacional Menéndez y Pelayo;
   Universidad de Alcalá
Further Reading El croquis, no. 81/82

**Carmen Martinez Arroyo, Emilio Pemjean Muñoz,
Rodrigo Pemjean Muñoz , Madrid** (see p. 122)
Award Winning Building Town Hall, Clinic and Meeting
   Room
Location Madarcos, Madrid, Spain
Design and Construction Period 1994–Dec. 1996
Award IV Bienal de Arquitectura Española
Given by Consejo Superior de los Colegios de
   Arquitectos de España; Ministerio de Fomento;
   Universidad Internacional Menéndez y Pelayo;
   Universidad de Alcalá
Further Reading AV Monografías 63–64, 1997

Joan Nogué, Txema Onzain, Jordi Roig, Barcelona
   (see p. 123)
Award Winning Building Nuns' Residence and Youth
   Hostel
Location Eguino, Alava, Spain
Design and Construction Period 1994–1996
Award IV Bienal de Arquitectura Española
Given by Consejo Superior de los Colegios de
   Arquitectos de España; Ministerio de Fomento;
   Universidad Internacional Menéndez y Pelayo;
   Universidad de Alcalá
Further Reading Magasin A + T, no. 9, 1997, ISSN
   1132–6409

Carlos Puente, Madrid
Award Winning Building Centro de Cultura de
   Ciempozuelos
Location Ciempozuelos, Madrid, Spain
Design and Construction Period 1993–1995
Award IV Bienal de Arquitectura Española
Given by Consejo Superior de los Colegios de
   Arquitectos de España; Ministerio de Fomento;
   Universidad Internacional Menéndez y Pelayo;
   Universidad de Alcalá
Further Reading El croquis, no. 76

Álvaro Siza Vieira, Porto (see p. 124)
Award Winning Building Jardim de Santo Domingo
   de Bonaval
Location Santiago de Compostela, Spain
Design and Construction Period 1989–1994
Award III Prémio Manuel de la Dehesa 1997
Given by IV Bienal de Arquitectura Española
Further Reading Magazine Lotus, no. 88 (Italy)

Tonet Sunyer i Vives, Barcelona (see p. 126)
Award Winning Building Sendín House
Location Madrid, Spain
Design and Construction Period 1993–1995
Award IV Bienal de Arquitectura Española
Given by Consejo Superior de los Colegios de
   Arquitectos de España; Ministerio de Fomento;
   Universidad Internacional Menéndez y Pelayo;
   Universidad de Alcalá
Further Reading El croquis, no. 76

Basilio Tobías, Zaragoza
Award Winning Building Hotel Ciudad de Zaragoza
Location Zaragoza, Spain
Design and Construction Period 1992–1995
Award IV Bienal de Arquitectura Española
Given by Consejo Superior de los Colegios de
   Arquitectos de España; Ministerio de Fomento;
   Universidad Internacional Menéndez y Pelayo;
   Universidad de Alcalá
Further Reading Revista Av, no. 63–64

Guillermo Vázquez Consuegra, Seville (see p. 128)
Award Winning Building Instituto Andaluz del
   Patrimonio Histórico
Location Seville, Spain
Design and Construction Period 1997
Award IV Bienal de Arquitectura Española
Given by Consejo Superior de los Colegios de
   Arquitectos de España; Ministerio de Fomento;
   Universidad Internacional Menéndez y Pelayo;
   Universidad de Alcalá
Further Reading A + U Architecture and Urbanism,
   December 1996, no. 315

**Ignacio Vicens y Hualde, José Antonio Ramos
Abengozar, Madrid** (see p. 130)
Award Winning Building Edificio de Ciencias Sociales
   de la Universidad de Navarra
Location Pamplona, Spain
Design and Construction Period 1994–1996
Award 1) IV Bienal de Arquitectura Española;
   2) Premios COAVN de Arquitectura
Given by 1) Consejo Superior de los Colegios de
   Arquitectos de España, Ministerio de Fomento,
   Universidad Internacional de Menéndez Pelayo,
   Universidad de Alcalá; 2) Colegio Oficial de
   Arquitectos Vasco Navarro

SWEDEN

HLT, Henning Larsens Tegnestue A/S, Kopenhagen
   (see p. 132)
Award Winning Building Malmö Stadsbibliotek
Location Malmö, Sweden
Design and Construction Period 1993–1998
Award Kasper Salin-priset 1997
Given by SAR Svenska Arkitekters Riksförbund
Further Reading 1) MAMA no. 18, February 1998;
   2) Magasin för modern arkitektur, Stockholm, Sweden

SWITZERLAND

Ackermann & Friedli, Basel
Award Winning Building Tagesschule Am Bachgraben
Location Allschwil, Switzerland
Design and Construction Period Jan. 1994–Oct. 1994
Award Prix Special Soprema 1997
Given by BNA Bond van Nederlandse Architekten,
   BDA Bund Deutscher Architekten Rheinland-Pfalz,
   Conseil National de l'Ordre des Architectes, BSA
Further Reading Werk, Bauen + Wohnen, no. 1/2,
   January/February 1996

UKRAINE

**Scientific Research Institute of Experimental Design
for Residential and Public Buildings, Kyiv**
Award Winning Building Town Slavutych
Location Slavutych, Kyiv Region, Ukraine
Design and Construction Period 1986–1996
Award 1997 Ukraine State Award in Architecture
Given by Union of Architects of Ukraine; Ukraine State
   Award in Architecture Presidential Committee

**Scientific Research Institute of Theory and History
of Architectural and Town Planning, Kyiv**
Award Winning Building The Historical Places, connected
   with Life and Activities of Bogdan Khmelnitsky in the
   first Hetman's Capital Chygryn and Family Residence
   of Subotov
Location Chygryn and Subotov, Cherkasy Region,
   Ukraine

Design and Construction Period 1992–1996
Award 1997 Ukraine State Award in Architecture
Given by Union of Architects of Ukraine; Ukraine State
   Award in Architecture Presidential Committee
Further Reading The Magazine Apxumekmypa u npec-
   music, 1997, no. 1–2, pp. 23–26; Magazine ACC,
   1997, no. 26, p. 37

UNITED KINGDOM

Alsop + Störmer Architects, London (see p. 134)
Award Winning Building Le Grand Bleu – Hôtel du
   Département des Bouches-du-Rhône
Location Marseille, France
Design and Construction Period 50 months
Award RIBA Architecture Award (Europe)
Given by RIBA The Royal Institute of British Architects
Further Reading Le Grand Bleu, Academy Editions

Armstrong Architects, London (see p. 136)
Award Winning Building La Maison de la Culture du
   Japon à Paris
Location Paris, France
Design and Construction Period 1992–1997
Award RIBA Architecture Award (Europe)
Given by RIBA The Royal Institute of British Architects
Further Reading Kenchiku Bunka, Vol. 52, no. 611,
   September 1997

ASH Sakula Architects, London
Award Winning Building Birdwing Conservatory
Location London, United Kingdom
Design and Construction Period 1994–1996
Award RIBA Regional Architecture Award (London)
Given by RIBA The Royal Institute of British Architects
Further Reading Wings of Glass, in: The Architects'
   Journal, cover and pp. 32–33

Bennetts Associates, London
Award Winning Building John Menzies Ltd.,
   Wholesale Division Headquarters
Location Edinburgh, Scotland, United Kingdom
Design and Construction Period Sept. 1993–Sept. 1995
Award RIBA Regional Architecture Award (Scotland)
Given by RIBA The Royal Institute of British Architects
Further Reading Architect's Journal, November/30/1995

CASS Associates, Liverpool
Award Winning Building Birkenhead Bus Station
Location Birkenhead, United Kingdom
Design and Construction Period Sept. 1994–March 1997
Award RIBA Regional Architecture Award (North West)
Given by RIBA The Royal Institute of British Architects
Further Reading Architects Journal, November 6, 1997

Feilden Clegg Architects, Roderick James, Bath
Award Winning Building The Olivier Theatre, Bedales
   School
Location Petersfield, Hampshire, United Kingdom
Design and Construction Period May 1995–Oct. 1996
Award RIBA Regional Architecture Award (Southern)
Given by RIBA The Royal Institute of British Architects
Further Reading Back in the Frame, Perspectives,
   February/March 1998

The Goddard Wybor Practice, Leeds (see p. 138)
Award Winning Building The Knavesmire Stand
Location York, United Kingdom
Design and Construction Period Jan. 1994–May 1996
Award RIBA Regional Architecture Award (Yorkshire)
Given by RIBA The Royal Institute of British Architects

Mark Guard Architects, London
Award Winning Building Rooftop Apartment
Location Paris, France
Award RIBA/Ibstock Award for Houses and Housing
   (Europe)
Given by RIBA The Royal Institute of British Architects
Further Reading 34 m² sur les toiles, Maison Madame
   Figaro, Printemps 97, p. 136

Nicholas Hare Architects, London (see p. 140)
Award Winning Building The Kempe Centre, Wye
   College, University of London
Location Wye, Kent, United Kingdom
Design and Construction Period September 1993–
   May 1996

Award RIBA Regional Architecture Award (South East)
Given by RIBA The Royal Institute of British Architects
Further Reading RIBA Journal, April 1997

MacCormac Jamieson Prichard, London (see p. 142)
Award Winning Building Trinity College, Cambridge: Burrell's Field Development
Location Cambridge, United Kingdom
Design and Construction Period October 1989– September 1995
Award RIBA Regional Architecture Award (Eastern)
Given by RIBA The Royal Institute of British Architects
Further Reading The Architectural Review, Volume CCI, no. 1204, June 1997, pp. 66–71

Richard Murphy Architects, Edinburgh
Award Winning Building Maggies Centre, Western General Hospital
Location Edinburgh, United Kingdom
Design and Construction Period January 1995– September 1996
Award RIBA Department of Health Architecture in Healthcare Award
Given by RIBA The Royal Institute of British Architects
Further Reading Architects Journal, March/13/1997

One Seventeen Ad, Huddersfield
Award Winning Building The Round House
Location Hall Bower, Huddersfield, United Kingdom
Design and Construction Period June 1994– December 1995
Award RIBA Regional Architecture Award (Yorkshire)
Given by RIBA The Royal Institute of British Architects
Further Reading Perspectives on Architecture, no. 23, June/July 1996, p. 60; Individual Homes, November 1996, p. 24

Shane O'Toole, Michael Kelly – Group 91 Architects, Dublin (see p. 144)
Award Winning Building The Ark – A Cultural Centre for Children
Location Temple Bar, Dublin, Ireland
Design and Construction Period 1992–1995
Award RIBA Architecture Award (Europe)
Given by RIBA The Royal Institute of British Architects
Further Reading Temple Bar: The Power of an Idea, The Temple Bar Properties, Dublin 1996

PCKO Architects, Middlesex
Award Winning Building Swansea Foyer
Location Alexandra Road, Swansea, Wales, United Kingdom
Award RIBA Regional Architecture Award (Wales)
Given by RIBA The Royal Institute of British Architects
Further Reading The Architect's Journal, June/19/1997

Penoyre & Prasad Architects, London
Award Winning Building Woodlands Nursing Home
Location Lambeth, London, United Kingdom
Design and Construction Period 1993–1995
Award RIBA Regional Architecture Award (London)
Given by RIBA The Royal Institute of British Architects
Further Reading RIBA Journal, November 1995

Sheppard Robson, London (see p. 146)
Award Winning Building The Helicon, 1 South Place
Location London, United Kingdom
Design and Construction Period September 1991– August 1996
Award RIBA Regional Architecture Award (London)
Given by RIBA The Royal Institute of British Architects
Further Reading The Helicon, London 1996

Stickland Coombe Architecture, London
Award Winning Building Sculpture Niche at No. 1 Elvaston Place
Location London, United Kingdom
Design and Construction Period 8 weeks
Award RIBA Regional Architecture Award (London)
Given by RIBA The Royal Institute of British Architects
Further Reading The Independent, October/2/1997

Michael Wilford and Partners with James Stirling, London (see p. 148)
Award Winning Building Music School
Location Stuttgart, Germany
Design and Construction Period 1986–1996
Award RIBA Architecture Award (Europe), The Stirling Prize
Given by RIBA The Royal Institute of British Architects

Further Reading Maxwell, Robert: Building: Formal inquiry: Stirling Wilford's Stuttgart Music School, in: Architecture Today, no. 72, London, October 1996, pp. 20–30

Chris Wilkinson Architects, London (see p. 150)
Award Winning Building Stratford Market Depot
Location Stratford, London, United Kingdom
Design and Construction Period May 1991–April 1996
Award RIBA Commercial Architecture Award
Given by RIBA The Royal Institute of British Architects
Further Reading Architectural Journal, July/31/1997– August/7/1997

Derek Wylie Architecture, London (see p. 152)
Award Winning Building Lee House
Location London, United Kingdom
Design and Construction Period 9 months
Award RIBA Regional Architecture Award (London)
Given by RIBA The Royal Institute of British Architects
Further Reading Pierre, Catherine: Patio à Londres, Le Moniteur Architecture AMC, Paris, June 1997, no. 223

USA

Renzo Piano Building Workshop, Genova
(see p. 154)
Representative Building Jean-Marie Tjibaou Cultural Centre
Location Noumea, New Caledonia
Design and Construction Period 1991–1998
Award 1998 Pritzker Architecture Prize
Given by The Hyatt Foundation
Further Reading Renzo Piano Logbook, London 1997

David Baker Associates Architects, San Francisco; Crosby Helmich Architects (see p. 156)
Award Winning Building Manville Hall Student Apartments
Location Berkeley, California, USA
Design and Construction Period 1992–1995
Award AIA National Honor Award for Architecture 1997
Given by AIA The American Institute of Architects
Further Reading Architectural Record, May 1997, p. 76

Bissell Architects, Newport Beach
Award Winning Building San Francisco Solano Catholic Church
Location Rancho Santa Margarita, California, USA
Design and Construction Period April 1944– March 1996
Award AIA Religious Art and Architecture Design Award 1998
Given by AIA The American Institute of Architects
Further Reading Faith & Form (AIA Journal of Religious Architecture)

Hugh A. Boyd, Architects, New York
Award Winning Building The Salad Bowl
Location New York, New York, USA
Design and Construction Period 1993
Award AIA National Honor Award for Interiors 1998
Given by AIA The American Institute of Architects
Further Reading Interior Design Magazine, Nov. 1993

Brayton & Hughes, Design Studio, San Francisco
(see p. 158)
Award Winning Building Boyd Lighting Headquarters
Location San Francisco, California, USA
Award AIA National Honor Award for Architecture 1997
Given by AIA The American Institute of Architects
Further Reading Architectural Record, May 1997

Brayton & Hughes, Design Studio, San Francisco
Award Winning Building St. Ignatius Church, Donor's Chapel
Location San Francisco, California, USA
Design and Construction Period 8 months
Award AIA Religious Art and Architecture Design Award 1998
Given by AIA The American Institute of Architects
Further Reading Faith & Form Magazine, March 1998

Conger Fuller Architects – Michael Fuller, Scott Broughton, Aspen
Award Winning Building Saint Benedict's Monastary Retreat Center
Location Old Snowmass, Pitkin County, Colorado, USA

Design and Construction Period 1991–1994
Award AIA Religious Art and Architecture Design Award 1997
Given by AIA The American Institute of Architects

François de Menil Architect, P.C., New York; Bergmeyer Associates, Inc., Boston (see p. 160)
Award Winning Building Bottega Veneta, The Copley Place Mall
Location Boston, Massachusetts, USA
Design and Construction Period May 1995–Nov. 1995
Award AIA National Honor Award for Interiors 1997
Given by AIA The American Institute of Architects
Further Reading Architectural Record, May 1996

Steven Ehrlich Architects, Santa Monica (see p. 161)
Award Winning Building Paul Cummins Library, Crossroads School
Location Santa Monica, California, USA
Design and Construction Period 1995–1996
Award AIA National Honor Award for Architecture 1997
Given by AIA The American Institute of Architects
Further Reading L'Arca, May 1997

Steven Ehrlich Architects, Santa Monica (see p. 162)
Award Winning Building Schulman Residence
Location Brentwood, California, USA
Design and Construction Period 1989–1992
Award AIA National Honor Award for Architecture 1997
Given by AIA The American Institute of Architects
Further Reading Monograph

Steven Ehrlich Architects, Santa Monica
Award Winning Building Sony Pictures Entertainment – Game Show, Network
Location Culver City, California, USA
Design and Construction Period 1992–1994
Award AIA National Honor Award for Architecture 1997
Given by AIA The American Institute of Architects
Further Reading Architectural Record, May 1997

Hammel Green and Abrahamson Inc., Minneapolis
Award Winning Building Holy Spirit Catholic Church
Location Rochester, Minnesota, USA
Design and Construction Period Jan. 1994–Aug. 1995
Award AIA Religious Art and Architecture Design Award 1998
Given by AIA The American Institute of Architects

Hugh Hardy – Hardy Holzman Pfeiffer Associates, New York (see p. 164)
Award Winning Building New Victory Theater
Location New York, New York, USA
Design and Construction Period opened 1995
Award AIA Honor Award for Interiors 1997
Given by AIA The American Institute of Architects

Herbert Lewis Kruse Blunck Architecture, Des Moines (see p. 166)
Award Winning Building Praxair Distribution, Inc.
Location Ankeny, Iowa, USA
Design and Construction Period Jan. 1996–Feb. 1997
Award AIA National Honor Award for Architecture 1997
Given by AIA The American Institute of Architects
Further Reading Architecture Magazine, May 1997; Architectural Record, May 1997

Herbert Lewis Kruse Blunck Architecture, Des Moines
Award Winning Building Meyocks and Priebe Advertising, Inc.
Location West Des Moines, Iowa, USA
Design and Construction Period Phase I: December 1994–June 1995; Phase II: March 1996–June 1996
Award AIA National Honor Award for Architecture 1997
Given by AIA The American Institute of Architects
Further Reading Architectural Record, May 1997

Malcolm Holzman (Hardy Holzman Pfeiffer Associates), New York
Award Winning Building Dillingham Hall at the Punahou School
Location Honolulu, Hawaii, USA
Award AIA Honor Award for Interiors 1997
Given by AIA The American Institute of Architects

Vincent James Associates Inc., Minneapolis (Project initiated by James/Snow Architects Inc.)
(see p. 168)
Award Winning Building Type/Variant House

Location   Northern Wisconsin, USA
Design and Construction Period   1994–1997
Award   AIA National Honor Award for Architecture 1998
Given by   AIA The American Institute of Architects
Further Reading   Northwoods Escape, in: Architecture Magazine, February 1997

KressCox Associates P.C., Washington, D.C.
(see p. 170)
Award Winning Building   Connelly Chapel of Holy Wisdom of the Washington Theological Union
Location   Washington, D.C., USA
Design and Construction Period   1994–1996
Award   AIA Religious Art and Architecture Design Award 1997
Given by   AIA The American Institute of Architects
Further Reading   Environment and Art December 1996; The Washington Post, May/24/1997

KressCox Associates P.C., Washington, D.C.
Award Winning Building   Chapel of the Sacred Heart – Convent Chapel, Georgetown Visitation Monastery
Location   Washington, D.C., USA
Design and Construction Period   1994–1996
Award   AIA Religious Art and Architecture Design Award 1998
Given by   AIA The American Institute of Architects

KressCox Associates, P.C., Washington, D.C.
Award Winning Building   Arlington Cemetery Facility Maintenance Complex
Location   Arlington, Virginia, USA
Design and Construction Period   1992–1995
Award   AIA National Honor Award for Architecture 1997
Given by   AIA The American Institute of Architects
Further Reading   The Washington Post, October/19/1996

KressCox Associates P.C., Washington, D.C.
Award Winning Building   Western Presbyterian Church
Location   Washington, D.C., USA
Design and Construction Period   1989–1995
Award   AIA Religious Art and Architecture Design Award 1997
Given by   AIA The American Institute of Architects
Further Reading   Architecture, November 1995

Leers Weinzapfel Associates, Boston   (see p. 172)
Award Winning Building   Massachusetts Institute of Technology School of Architecture and Planning
Location   Cambridge, Massachusetts, USA
Design and Construction Period   1994–1988
Award   AIA National Honor Award for Interiors 1998
Given by   AIA The American Institute of Architects
Further Reading   Artful Chesion, Architecture, Aug. 1996

Edward I. Mills and Associates + Perkins Eastman and Partners, New York   (see p. 174)
Award Winning Building   Temple Beth Shalom Synagogue
Location   Hastings-on-Hudson, New York, USA
Design and Construction Period   completed 1995
Award   AIA Religious Art and Architecture Design Award 1997
Given by   AIA The American Institute of Architects
Further Reading   Temple Beth Shalom, Faith and Form, Volume 30, no. 1, 1997

Moore Ruble Yudell Architects & Planners, Santa Monica
Award Winning Building   Powell Library Renovation and Addition, University of California
Location   Los Angeles, California, USA
Design and Construction Period   1990–1996
Award   AIA National Honor Award for Architecture 1998
Given by   AIA The American Institute of Architects
Further Reading   By the book, in: Architecture, March 1997

PMG Architects – Peter M. Gumpel, New York; in Association with STARCK – Philippe Starck, Issy Les Moulineaux, France   (see p. 176)
Award Winning Building   Delano Hotel
Location   Miami Beach, Florida, USA
Award   AIA National Honor Award for Architecture 1997
Given by   AIA The American Institute of Architects

Roth and Moore Architects, New Haven   (see p. 177)
Award Winning Building   Joseph Slifka Center for Jewish Life at Yale
Location   New Haven, Connecticut, USA
Design and Construction Period   1964–1995

Award   AIA Religious Art and Architecture Design Award 1997
Given by   AIA The American Institute of Architects

Salmela Architect – David D. Salmela, Duluth
(see p. 178)
Award Winning Building   Brandenburg's Ravenwood Studio
Location   Ely, Minnesota, USA
Design and Construction Period   1995–1997
Award   AIA National Honor Award for Architecture 1998
Given by   AIA The American Institute of Architects
Further Reading   Architecture Magazine, May 1997; Architectural Record, May 1998

Mark Simon – Centerbrook Architects and Planners LLC, Essex
Award Winning Building   New Hearth Showroom
Location   New York, New York, USA
Design and Construction Period   June 1996–April 1997
Award   AIA National Honor Award for Interior 1998
Given by   AIA The American Institute of Architects
Further Reading   The New York Times Magazine, A Moveable Feat, Sunday March 30, 1997

Skidmore, Owings & Merrill LLP, San Francisco
(see p. 180)
Award Winning Building   United States Court of Appeals
Location   San Francisco, California, USA
Design and Construction Period   1990–1995
Award   1) AIA National Honor Award for Architecture 1998; 2) AIA National Honor Awards for Interiors 1998
Given by   AIA The American Institute of Architects
Further Reading   Betsky Aaron: Preservation Technology: Isolated Grandeur, Architecture Magazine, July 1997, pp. 146–152

Daniel Solomon and Gary Strang Architects with Philip C. Rossington, San Francisco   (see p. 182)
Award Winning Building   Beth Israel Memorial Chapel and Garden
Location   Houston, Texas, USA
Design and Construction Period   1993–February 1997
Award   AIA Religious Art and Architecture Design Award 1998
Given by   AIA The American Institute of Architects

Studio E Architects, San Diego   (see p. 184)
Award Winning Building   Orange Place Cooperative
Location   Escondido, California, USA
Design and Construction Period   2 years
Award   AIA National Honor Award for Architecture 1998
Given by   AIA The American Institute of Architects
Further Reading   Architectural Record (US), May 1998

TAMS Consultants Inc. Architects, Engineers & Planners (Joint Venture of TAMS/URS/Gannett Fleming), Boston; Wallace, Floyd, Associates, Inc. & Stull and Lee, Inc. (Joint Venture of Bechtell and Parsons Brinkerhoff)   (see p. 186)
Award Winning Building   Ventilation Building/ Ted Williams Tunnel
Location   Logan International Airport, Boston, Massachusetts, USA
Design and Construction Period   1990–1997
Award   AIA National Honor Award for Architecture 1998
Given by   AIA The American Institute of Architects
Further Reading   Architectural Record, February 1998

Westfourth Architecture P.C., New York   (see p. 188)
Award Winning Building   101 Cityfood Cafe
Location   New York, New York, USA
Design and Construction Period   July 1996–June 1997
Award   AIA National Honor Award for Interiors 1998
Given by   AIA The American Institute of Architects
Further Reading   Space Architecture Arst Design, March 1998, vol. 364

Chris Wilkinson Architects, London   (see p. 190)
Award Winning Building   South Quay Footbridge
Location   London, United Kingdom
Design and Construction Period   completed May 1997
Award   AIA Award for Excellence in Design 1997
Given by   AIA The American Institute of Architects
Further Reading   L'Arca, March 1998

Williams & Dynerman Architects, Washington, D.C.
(see p. 192)
Award Winning Building   The Henri Beaufour Institute
Location   Washington, D.C., USA
Design and Construction Period   Oct. 1991–Feb. 1993
Award   AIA National Honor Award for Architecture 1997
Given by   AIA The American Institute of Architects

Tod Williams Billie Tsien and Associates, New York
(see p. 194)
Award Winning Building   The Neurosciences Institute
Location   La Jolla, California, USA
Design and Construction Period   1992–1995
Award   AIA National Honor Award for Architecture 1997
Given by   AIA The American Institute of Architects
Further Reading   Global Architectura Document 50, May 1997

Ziger/Snead Architects, Baltimore
Award Winning Building   Brown Memorial Woodbrook Presbyterian Church
Location   Baltimore, Maryland, USA
Design and Construction Period   1991–1994
Award   AIA Religious Art and Architecture Design Award 1997
Given by   AIA The American Institute of Architects
Further Reading   Faith & Form (AIA Journal of Religious Architecture)

Zimmer Gunsul Frasca Partnership, Seattle
(see p. 196)
Award Winning Building   Bellevue Regional Library
Location   Bellevue, Washington, USA
Design and Construction Period   Feb. 1991–Feb. 1993
Award   AIA National Honor Award for Architecture 1997
Given by   AIA The American Institute of Architects
Further Reading   Zimmer Gunsul Frasca: Building Community

Indexes

Architects
of AWA 1996, 1997 and 1998

211

Building Types

I – Public buildings

1) Museums/Visitor centers
2) Cultural buildings
3) Education and Research buildings
4) Libraries
5) Hospitals/Medical care centers/ Laboratories
6) Churches/Convents/Religious buildings/Synagogues
7) Transport facilities
8) Public administration buildings
9) Miscellaneous

II – Office/Administration buildings

III – Industrial buildings

IV – Residential buildings

1) Private houses
2) Apartment buildings
3) Housing complexes/Urban planning
4) Old Peoples Home

V – Hotels/Hostels/Restaurants/ Cafés/Night Clubs

VI – Commercial buildings

I – Public buildings

1) Museums/Visitor centers

Prestel books are available worldwide.
Please contact your nearest bookseller
or write to either of the following
addresses for information concerning
your local distributor:

Prestel Verlag, Mandlstrasse 26,
D-80802 Munich, Germany
Phone (89) 38 17 09-0,
Fax (89) 38 17 09-35

Prestel Verlag, 16 West 22nd Street,
New York, N.Y. 10010, USA
Phone (212) 6278199,
Fax (212) 6279866

Library of Congress Cataloging-in-
Publication Data is available.

Die Deutsche Bibliothek –
CIP-Einheitsaufnahme
Award Winning Architecture ... :
AWA; international yearbook ...
- Engl. Orig-Ausg. – Munich;
New York: Prestel.
Erscheint jährl. – Aufnahme nach 1996
ISSN 1430-9459
NE: AWA ; international yearbook ...
Engl. Orig. – Ausg.
1996 –

Translation of the editors' forewords:
Peter Green

Editorial coordination: Bettina
Schimmer, Diana Wessling

Design: WIGEL, Munich
Offset lithography: ReproLine, Munich
Printing and binding: Offizin Andersen
Nexö, Leipzig

Printed on acid-free paper

ISBN 3-7913-1992-2
ISSN 1430-9459